WONDERS OF LO

The Artistic Heritage
of Mustang

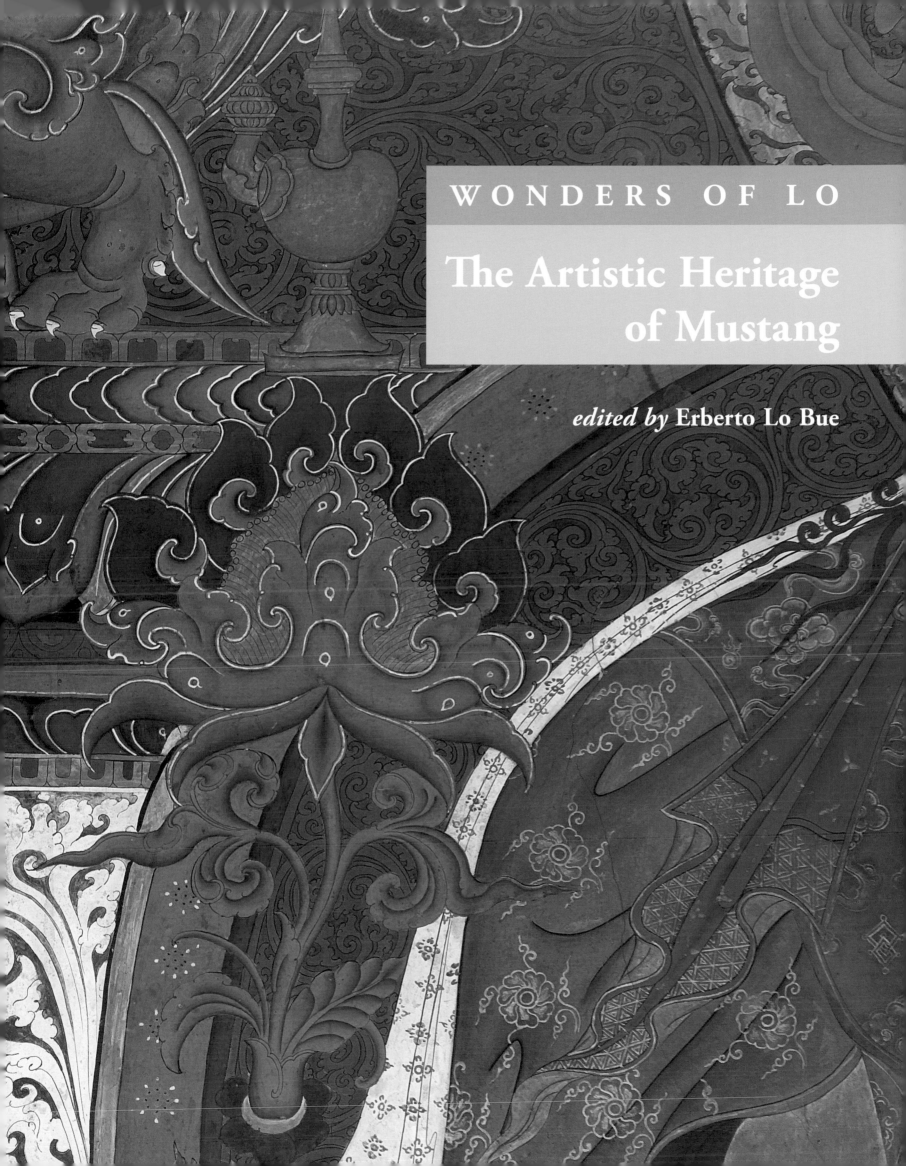

WONDERS OF LO

The Artistic Heritage
of Mustang

edited by Erberto Lo Bue

This book has been made possible
by support received from
MOONSAIL INTERNATIONAL
HOLDING S.A.

General Editor
PRATAPADITYA PAL

Senior Executive Editor
SAVITA CHANDIRAMANI
Senior Editorial Executive
ARNAVAZ K. BHANSALI
Editorial Executive
RAHUL D'SOUZA

Text Editor
RIVKA ISRAEL

Designer
NAJU HIRANI
Senior Production Executive
GAUTAM V. JADHAV
Production Executive
VIDYADHAR R. SAWANT

Vol. 62 No. 2
December 2010
Price: ₹ 2500.00 / US$ 68.00
ISBN: 978-93-80581-02-6
Library of Congress Catalog Card Number:
2010-319020

Published by Radhika Sabavala for The Marg Foundation at
Army & Navy Building (3rd Floor), 148, M.G. Road, Mumbai 400 001, India.
Printed at Silverpoint Press Pvt. Ltd., Navi Mumbai and Processed at
The Marg Foundation, Mumbai.

For captions to the illustrations on jacket, endpapers, and preliminary pages,
see figures 9.6, 8.12, 9.3, 9.7, 7.2, 6.8, 9.12, 5.6, 11.10, and 7.1.

**Marg's quarterly publications receive support from the
Sir Dorabji Tata Trust – Endowment Fund**

CONTENTS

Preface

This is the first monograph on the art of Lo, as Mustang is called by its inhabitants. It deals with the most important and some hitherto unpublished sites in the region, with a special emphasis on painting, in which Lo excelled. The area has maintained a degree of autonomy, avoiding the Fifth Dalai Lama's take-over of Tibet and, thanks to its inclusion in the Gorkha kingdom, Chinese colonization as well as the disasters of the Cultural Revolution.

Buddhism, along with other important features of Indian culture, was introduced into Lo by Indian and Tibetan masters, especially through the translations of Sanskrit texts, while aesthetics of Indian origin were introduced by Newar and Tibetan artists through the consistent use of Indian iconography and iconometry.

Arts flourished in Lo particularly during the 15th century, under rulers favouring the religious order of Sakya, in southwest Tibet. What is left of the region's artistic treasures was in a poor state of preservation by the time the Italian scholar Giuseppe Tucci visited Lo, in 1952. Since 1999 important restoration work has been carried out in two temples at Möntang, the main town in Lo, thanks to the sponsorship of the American Himalayan Foundation.

This publication would not have been possible without Luigi Fieni's generous cooperation and unfaltering assistance during and after the fieldwork we carried out with two other contributors to this volume – Amy Heller, whom I thank for several suggestions, and Chiara Bellini, a former PhD student of mine – in the company of my trek mate, Luciano Monticelli. I am grateful to Dr Pratapaditya Pal for taking into consideration and accepting the project of this book, to the University of Bologna for sponsoring my fieldwork, and to Ferruccio Abbiati and Marco Pilati for contributing to the publication of the volume. Thanks are due also to David Jackson for reading chapter 3 and giving useful advice on it. I dedicate my editorial work to the memory of a former student, collaborator, and friend of mine, Leonardo Gribaudo (1949–2007), who passed away after his return from a last trek in Nepal.

The phonetic transcription of Tibetan words in the volume follows the system adopted by the Tibetan and Himalayan Digital Library, whereas the corresponding transliterations are listed at the end of the volume.

Erberto Lo Bue

SOUTHWEST TIBET

NEPAL
LO
Kathmandu
INDIA

Rindzinling
Könchokling
TSOSHAR
Chödzong
Möntang
Samdrupling
Lo Gekar
Tsarang
Yara
Luri
Trashi Geling

DOLPO

Gemi
Tangye
Geling
Samar
Chele
Gönpa Khang
Tsukzang
Te
Tangbe

Kali Gandaki

Kagbeni
Dzong
Dzar
Muktinath
Khyingga
Lubrak
Jomsom

MANANG

Dhaulagiri
Nilgiri

N

Annapurna

LO (MUSTANG)

Not to scale

CHAPTER I

An Introduction to the Cultural
History of Lo (Mustang)

Erberto Lo Bue

Mustang is the name given by non-local people to a district and town in southwest geo-cultural Tibet, which have been part of the Gorkha kingdom since the 18th century and are now included in the Dhaulagiri zone of northwest Nepal. The actual names of the region and of its main town, lying on a small plain at 3,809 metres above sea level, are Lo and Möntang respectively. The district has an area of 2,563 square kilometres and counts almost 1,200 households for a total of over 6,000 resident people, both indigenous and Tibetan, mostly devoted to agriculture and cattle breeding. They grow chiefly barley and buckwheat, while raising goats, sheep, horses, mules, and yaks as well as their breeds, totalling around 41,000 heads, with a ratio of about seven animals per person. Lo is extremely dry, for the monsoon rains hardly reach the area of the Tibetan plateau where it lies, and has to rely almost exclusively upon glacier streams for its water supply.

Besides agriculture and animal husbandry, trade has represented an important source of livelihood in Lo, thanks to its strategic position north of the Himalayan range and its control over the passes linking the Brahmaputra basin, in Tibet, with the Kali Gandaki Valley, in Nepal. The Kali Gandaki river flows through Lo from north to south, forming one of the deepest canyons in the world, partly corresponding to one of the main trade and pilgrim routes across the Himalaya, linking southwest Tibet to India via Nepal. Lower Lo is now crossed by a dirt road leading to the sanctuary of Muktinath, which is the object of intense pilgrimage by Hindu and Buddhist devotees from Nepal and India. The route proceeds towards Upper Lo from the ancient border town of Kak (Kagbeni), a Tibetan word meaning "obstacle" and referring to its strategic position in the middle of the path at a narrower point of the river (figure 1.1). After leaving the Kali Gandaki, the path divides into several routes which join again at Möntang, from where it continues towards the counties of Drongpa and Saga, roughly corresponding to the ancient Tibetan kingdom of Gungtang.

During his pioneer visit to the region in October 1952 Giuseppe Tucci (1894–1984), the first scholar who tried to piece together some of the main events in the history of Lo, noticed groups of Tibetan pilgrims travelling towards Nepal and India to visit their holy Buddhist sites. He remarked that, in spite of its apparent shabbiness, Möntang was still rich thanks to active trade with Tibet and predicted that, owing to political reasons, one day the border would be closed with checkpoints. That happened ten years later, following the Chinese occupation of Tibet, but now trade is active again on an even greater scale than before, facilitated by a dirt carriage road connecting Möntang to the Tibetan border. Lo benefits from such trade, which makes some indispensable items cheaper and easier to obtain than those arriving from Nepal and India.

1.1 Kagbeni with its monastery seen from the north. Photograph: Luciano Monticelli.

Despite the great political changes that have occurred both in Tibet and in Nepal during the last 50 years, Lo remains one of the few Himalayan areas where features which are peculiar to traditional Tibetan culture have been preserved without interruption since the earliest historical times: language, writing, religion, diet, and social features including mutual assistance associations, polyandry, sky and water burial, as well as discrimination towards low-caste people such as blacksmiths, who have to live outside the main town.

Relatively little is known of the history of Lo before the 14th century, although in 651 CE the region was part of the Tibetan empire. One of the many copies of a famous wooden statue of Avalokiteshvara (figure 1.2), the tutelary bodhisattva of the first historical king of Tibet, kept in the Potala palace at Lhasa, is housed in the royal chapel in the palace of the rulers of Lo at Tsarang, south of Möntang (figure 1.3). The earliest Buddhist master to visit Lo was the famous tantric guru and magician Padmasambhava, a native of the Swat Valley, who moved to the Nepal Valley and was then invited to contribute to the foundation of the first Buddhist monastery in Tibet, Samyè, erected between 767 and 779. Images of Padmasambhava are often found in the monasteries of Lo and one of his most remarkable metal portraits is preserved at Lo Gekar (figure 1.4). Padmasambhava's relationship with Lo is recorded in two of the 108 cantos making up the *Pema tang-yik* (1352), the famous Tibetan religious epic devoted to his deeds.

During the 11th century Upper Lo was visited by Tibetan masters from southwest Tibet, including the famous yogin and poet Milarepa (1040–1123), who spent a summer there, near a lake, as we learn from the collection of his religious songs edited by another famous tantric yogin,

Tsang Nyön Heruka (1452–1507), who belonged to Milarepa's tantric tradition, known as Kagyü. Tsang Nyön edited Milarepa's biography (1488) between two visits to Lo (1481 and 1498), where he witnessed the war waged by the latter against Western Tibet and even negotiated a ceasefire between the two kingdoms.

By the 11th century another esoteric religious tradition was certainly practised in Lo: Bön, a belief system often confused with the indigenous religion of Tibet, which was based on the cult of royal tombs and sacrifices, and disappeared after the collapse of the Tibetan empire. The founder of Bön was not a Tibetan, and indeed the core of its doctrines and its

1.2 Avalokiteshvara. Tsarang palace, 17th century. Wood. Photograph: Tom Laird.

1.3 Buckwheat fields at Tsarang, with the
palace and monastery in the background.
Photograph: Chiara Bellini.

iconography (the general aspect of deities and many words making up their names, as well as their proportions, mudras/gestures, asanas/postures, colours, attributes) largely derive from Indian concepts, to the extent that Bön may be regarded as a heterodox form of Buddhism, not unlike the Nyingma tantric tradition spread by Padmasambhava's followers during the early diffusion of Buddhism in Tibet.

A Bön master from Lo, Ronggom Tokmé Zhikpo, was famous enough to attract a Tibetan disciple, Sherap Gyeltsen, whose second son, Trashi Gyeltsen (1131?–1215?) (figure 1.5), established a religious community at Lubrak that still represents the most important Bön centre in Lower Lo. The portraits of father and son are painted in the assembly hall of the hermitage of Gönpuk, which was built over a small cave where Trashi Gyeltsen had

1.4 Padmasambhava. Lo Gekar monastery, 15th century. Brass. Photograph: Luigi Fieni.

1.5 Trashi Gyeltsen. Gönpuk, c. 1997.
Distemper. Photograph: Chiara Bellini.

meditated for nine years, and was restored in 1997. Those murals, painted in 2002, are discussed by Chiara Bellini in chapter 10.

During the 11th century Lo – except for an invasion from Ladakh – was ruled by the kings of Western Tibet, who re-established Buddhism on orthodox grounds inviting Atisha Dipankara Srijnana (980–1054), the retired chancellor of the famous Indian university of Vikramashila, for that purpose. There is no evidence in Lo of the activity of that adventurous scholar, but it is conceivable that he crossed the region on his way to Western Tibet, which he reached in 1042. One of his main disciples, Tönpa Yang-rap, was from Lo. Around 1214 Lo was visited by the Kashmiri scholar Shakyashribhadra, the last abbot of Vikramashila, travelling home after a long stay in Tibet. However, the progress of Buddhism in Lo was slow and it was only in the early 14th century that the Nyingma lama Sanggyè Zangpo put an end to the slaughter of animals for sacrificial purposes there. An authoritative Tibetan historical source reports that there was a practice of cremating half a dozen men alive whenever a man died until, in the 14th century, the Kagyü lama Jampel Senggé preached the Buddhist doctrine to the Thakur ruler of southern Lo and the latter started regarding the representatives of the Kagyü order as protectors of his kingdom.

In spite of the prestige enjoyed by Nyingma, Bön, and Kagyü masters in Lo, their small communities in the area never grew to become important monastic centres. The religious order that eventually established its religious and cultural supremacy in Lo was based at the huge monastic fortress of Sakya, in southwest Tibet. Thanks to their status as vassals of the Yuan dynasty, the princely abbots of Sakya dominated much of southern Tibet from the mid-13th to the mid-14th century, but their cultural hegemony in Upper Lo was already felt since the 12th century, following Lama Ronggom's stay at Samdrupling, a monastery discussed by Maie Kitamura in chapter 11.

During the 13th century Lo made its contribution to the later diffusion of tantric Buddhism in Tibet in the person of a fine scholar, Sherap Rinchen (fl. mid-13th century), who was a disciple of the siddha Darpana-acharya and of Ravinda,[1] and became the religious preceptor of the famous Sakya scion Pakpa (1235–80), who in turn became Qubilai Khan's preceptor.

1.6 Khachö fort, 15th century. Photograph: Luigi Fieni.

In collaboration with the Indian pandita, Jayananda, Sherap Rinchen
translated five texts later included in the Tibetan canonical collection known
as *Tengyur*, two of which survive in monasteries of the Nepal Valley.² During
the latter half of the 13th and much of the 14th century Lo was ruled by the
kings of Gungtang, who had close ties with Sakya and who built a fort at
Muktinath, presumably to counter the influence of the rulers of Jumla.

After a period of struggle, the kingdom of Gungtang reasserted its
control over Lo during the last decades of the 14th century thanks to a
general, Sherap Lama, who established both secular and Buddhist laws in
his capacity as governor of the region. His family belonged to a branch
of the Tibetan Khyungpo clan, which supplied high officials to the rulers
of Gungtang, and to which several Bön and Buddhist masters, including
Milarepa, belonged. His younger son, Chökyongbum, reconquered the
Western Tibetan region of Purang in the 1380s and, as a reward, the
dharmaraja ("righteous ruler", Tibetan *chögyel*) of Gungtang appointed
him governor of the frontier fortress of Tsarang entrusting him with the
governance of Lo and neighbouring Dölpo.

Chökyongbum's son and successor, Amapel (1388–1447), extended
Lo's rule again to Purang as well as to other areas of Western Tibet and, in
order to assert his total control over the region, he had two members of a
rival family murdered by his attendants during a joint visit to a spa. Under
this aggressive ruler, Lo gained its independence from Gungtang, and rose to
greater importance and prosperity taking advantage of its strategic position.
Having become the first king of Lo, Amapel left his family's headquarters
at Tsarang and established new ones in the boat-shaped fortress of Khachö
(figure 1.6), just north of Möntang, where he built a palace.

As we have seen, Lo seems to have been resistant to the introduction
of organized forms of Buddhism until the 14th century and according to a
local scholar, Sönam Lhündrup (1456–1532), service towards religion lapsed
for a certain period until the time of Amapel. In spite of his ruthlessness
and perhaps also in order to make up for it, in conformity with Buddhist
practice, the latter strongly supported Buddhism, inviting two important
Tibetan masters to Lo. The most successful one was Künga Zangpo (1382–
1456), a leading figure within the Sakya order and the founder of the famous
monastery of Ngor, in southwest Tibet (1429). One of the greatest scholars in
15th-century Tibet, Künga Zangpo visited Lo on three different occasions,
and it was thanks to his and Amapel's concerted efforts that Buddhism was
established on an institutional basis in the region during the 15th century.

On the occasion of his first visit, in 1427, Künga Zangpo restored
the monastic college of Tsarang, consecrating its main building and
murals illustrating 12 mandalas of the yoga class. As witnessed by Tucci,
the monastery of Tsarang was in a state of decadence by the mid-20th
century and there was no abbot for its 33 monks at the time of my visit
in September 2008. Thanks to Amapel's sponsorship, Künga Zangpo
founded the monastery of Drakar Tekchenling near Möntang, establishing
a great seminary there, and finally ordained the king, who had secured his

succession by then. In 1429 another Sakya master, Tenpè Gyeltsen, founded
a fort-like monastery at the strategic site of Kak (figure 1.1), thus extending
the influence of his order further south. Statues of different periods and in
various sizes, materials, and styles – Tibetan as well as Newar – are kept
in that monastery (figures 1.7–1.9), whereas the clay image of a local pre-
Buddhist protecting deity, known as "Memé" ("Grandfather"), is housed in a
small courtyard near the northern entrance of the townlet (figure 1.10).

On the occasion of his second visit to Lo, in 1436, Künga Zangpo
consecrated a golden image of Vajradhara at the monastery of Drakar, built
a temple devoted to Chakrasamvara, and apparently laid the foundations of
the Golden Temple, later known as Maitreya temple (Jampa Lhakhang), at

1.7 Sakya Lama. Kagbeni monastery.
Photograph: Luciano Monticelli.

Möntang. Furthermore he had the
old monastery of Namgyel, about
3 kilometres northwest of Möntang,
repaired (figure 1.11) and laid the
foundations of the monastic centre
of Tupten Dargyeling at Tsarang.
Amapel had a great number of
sacred images and stupas made,
and is regarded as a manifestation
of Padmasambhava in a Nyingma
"prophecy" and referred to as
"Bodhisattva Dharmaraja" in local
historical sources.

His son and successor, the
dharmaraja Agön Zangpo (1420–
c. 1482), continued the territorial
expansion of Lo, invited Künga
Zangpo again, and honoured the
future third abbot of Ngor as his
chief preceptor. During his third
stay, from 1447 to 1449, Künga
Zangpo inspected the statue of
Maitreya as well as many other
images and was appointed by
the king as first abbot of Tupten
Dargyeling, which must have
become an important monastery
in Lo thanks to the endowment
of many estates. Agön Zangpo
also completed the monastery of
Drakar and the temple of Maitreya
mentioned above. The latter became
part of an overall urban project by
the king, who had a new palace
constructed in Möntang and the

1.8 Ratnasambhava. Kagbeni monastery, 15th century. Gilded copper. Photograph: Amy Heller.

1.9 Vajradhara. Kagbeni monastery, 15th century. Brass. Photograph: Luciano Monticelli.

capital surrounded with walls in 1441 (figure 1.12) following the model of the monastic fortress of Sakya, similarly built on flat land, and eventually left the castle of Khachö. The circumstance that Agön Zangpo shifted his residence from the hill to the plain suggests that he felt strong enough to rule his kingdom from a less strategic position, in contrast with the choices by then prevailing in geo-cultural Tibet.

Agön Zangpo's son and successor, Tsangchen Trashigön (c. 1445–89) extended his territories at the expense of the kingdom of Western Tibet and honoured the fourth abbot of Ngor (see figures 7.1 and 7.2) and other scholars as well as yogins as his religious preceptors. He sponsored the construction of the temple of Mahamuni (Tupchen Lhakhang) at Möntang (1468–72) and of a monastery at Gemi, completed the construction of the monastery of Tupten Dargyeling, and commissioned a large number of fine religious images and stupas.

The king's brother, the mahapandita ("great scholar") of Lo (1456–1532; see figures 7.6 and 7.7), became the abbot of the monastery of Tsarang, in conformity with one of the systems devised by Tibetan rulers to keep both secular and religious power within the same family. During that period scholars not only from Tibet, but also from the Nepal Valley, India, and Sri Lanka visited Lo, some of them carrying out translation activities there. The second half of the 15th and first half of the 16th century saw the birth of two more scholars, who became famous also in Tibet: the Nyingma master Pema Wangyel Dorjé (1487–1542), known as "mahapandita of Western Tibet" (see figure 7.5), and Jonang Künga Drölchok (1507–66). The former travelled also to the Nepal Valley, where he attended on Newar gurus.

Several rulers of Lo are remembered as having sponsored the making of sacred images and stupas, the construction of new monasteries and renovation of existing ones, as well as the copying and writing of religious texts. During the last two decades of the 16th century Döndrup Dorjé (ruled c. 1580–94) restored the monastery of Lo Gekar and built a new palace at Tsarang, where his successor Samdrup Dorjé (ruled c. 1594–1610) had a new main monastic building erected and decorated with excellent murals, commissioning many other paintings and statues.

The latter half of the 17th century saw a decline in the power of Lo in favour of the rulers of Jumla and of the kings of Ladakh, who attacked the fort of Kak. Friendly relations with Ladakh were restored through the marriages of the Ladakhi king's daughter with the king of Lo around 1700, and of the latter's sister with the son and future successor of the same Ladakhi king in 1723.

The last king of independent Lo, Wangyel Dorjé (c. 1738–c. 1795), supported both the Sakya and the Nyingma schools, restored the monastery of Gekar again, and built or renovated several other temples and monasteries, including Samdrupling, sponsoring the making of religious images and stupas. That activity was made possible by a period of peace and relative affluence that did not end in 1788, when the king pledged to become a tributary of the Gorkha ruler, in spite of his friendly relationship with the

1.10 "Grandfather Memé". Kagbeni. Clay and wood. Photograph: Luciano Monticelli.

1.11 Namgyel monastery. Photograph: Luciano Monticelli.

emperor of China, who succeeded in chasing the Gorkhas from Tibet in 1792 and bestowed an official name, rank, as well as insignia upon him. Under Nepalese administration Lo retained a degree of autonomy and, after over three centuries of wars fought against southern and northern rivals, enjoyed a long period of peace until 1961, when it was occupied by Tibetan guerrillas fighting against the Chinese army. The local population had to suffer from that occupation until 1974.

Wangyel Dorjé's descendants still bear the title of "raja", though in October 2008, following the proclamation of the federal republic of Nepal in May, they lost the last privileges they enjoyed. The present raja, Jikmé Dorjé Dradül, is married to a Tibetan lady, and the horses in his stable are of Tibetan stock. Whereas a fine green-enamelled cast-iron stove with a plate in French occupies a central position in the private chapel of his palace at Möntang, Tibetan and Chinese goods now flood the shops in town. Writings in both Chinese and Tibetan appear, as on a lorry abandoned in a fenced field southeast of the town. A motorable road reaches and now goes beyond Gemi, and since about 2003 dozens of lorries coming from Tibet have unloaded tons of goods on the occasion of fairs held two or three times a year at Möntang or in a village about one-hour's walk from it, or even at the border.

While commercial activity has once again resumed, cultural patterns in Lo are changing inexorably. The new prosperity might not revive the

1.12 Möntang. Photograph: Luigi Fieni.

brilliant artistic phase of the past which is the subject of this volume, but the increased religious activity, including concerted efforts to restore the painted, sculptural, and architectural treasures, should contribute to ensure that Lo and Möntang are no longer forgotten or neglected.

REFERENCES

Cordier, Palmyr. *Catalogue du Fonds Tibétain de la Bibliotèque Nationale: Index du Bstan-ḥgyur*, part III. Paris: Ernest Leroux, 1915.

Dhungel, Ramesh K. *The Kingdom of Lo (Mustang): A Historical Study*. Kathmandu: Tashi Gephel Foundation, 2002.

Dudjom Rinpoche, Jikdrel Yeshe Dorje. *The Nyingma School of Tibetan Buddhism: Its Fundamentals and History*, ed. Gyurme Dorje and Matthew Kapstein, vol. I: *The Translations*. Boston: Wisdom Publications, 1991.

'Gos lo gZhon nu dpal, *Deb ther sngon po*, vol. I. Chengdu: Si-khron Mi-rigs dPe-skrun-khang, 1984.

Gutschow, Niels and Charles Ramble. "Up and down, inside and outside: notions of space and territory in Tibetan villages of Mustang". *Sacred Landscapes of the Himalaya*, ed. Niels Gutschow, Axel Michaels, Charles Ramble, and Ernst Steinkellner. Vienna: Austrian Academy of Science Press, 2003.

Jackson, David P. *The Mollas of Mustang: Historical, Religious and Oratorical Traditions of the Nepalese-Tibetan Borderland*. Dharamsala: Library of Tibetan Works & Archives, 1984.

Jackson, David P. "A genealogy of the kings of Lo (Mustang)". *Tibetan Studies in Honour of Hugh Richardson*, ed. Michael Aris and Aung San Suu Kyi. Warminster: Aris & Phillips, 1980.

Jackson, David P. "Notes on the History of Se-rib, and Nearby Places in the Upper Kali Gandaki". *Kailash*, VI/3, 1978.

Jackson, David P. "The early history of Lo (Mustang) and Ngari". *Contributions to Nepalese Studies*, 4/1, 1976.

Kramer, Jowita. *A Noble Abbot from Mustang: Life and Works of Glo- bo mKhan-chen (1456–1532)*. Wien: Arbeitskreis für Tibetische und Buddhistische Studien, Universitet Wien, 2008.

Matthiessen, Peter. *East of Lo Monthang: In the Land of Mustang*. Boston: Shambhala, 1996.

Petech, Luciano. *The Kingdom of Ladakh: c. 950–1842 AD*. Roma: IsMEO, 1977.

Ramble, Charles and Marietta Kind. "Bonpo monasteries and temples of the Himalayan region". *A Survey of Bonpo Monasteries and Temples in Tibet and the Himalaya*, ed. Samten G. Karmay and Yasuhiko Nagano. Osaka: National Museum of Ethnology, 2003.

Roerich, George N. (ed.). *The Blue Annals*. Varanasi/Delhi: Motilal Banarsidass, 1976.

Snellgrove, David L. *Himalayan Pilgrimage*. Boulder: Prajña Press, 1981.

Snellgrove, David L. "Places of Pilgrimage in Thag (Thakkhola)". *Kailash*, VII/2, 1979.

Tucci, Giuseppe. *Tra giungle e pagode*. Roma: Newton Compton, 1979.

Tucci, Giuseppe. *Preliminary Report on Two Scientific Expeditions in Nepal*. Roma: IsMEO, 1956.

Vitali, Roberto. "On Byams pa and Thub chen lha khang of Glo sMos thang". *The Tibet Journal*, XXIV/1, 1999.

Vitali, Roberto (ed.). *The Kingdoms of Gu.ge Pu.hrang, according to mNga'. ris rgyal.rabs by Gu.ge mkhan.chen Ngag.dbang.grags.pa*. Dharamsala: Go.srig Tshog.chung, 1996.

NOTES

1   "Rebenda" in 'Gos lo gZhon nu dpal, *Deb ther sngon po*, Chengdu, 1984, vol. I, p. 460.

2   One of them at Svayambhu (cf. P. Cordier, *Catalogue du Fonds Tibétain de la Bibliotèque Nationale. Index du Bstan-ḥgyur*, part III, Paris, 1915, pp. 271, LXXXVI/92, and 477–80, CXXIII/14, 17, 19, and 22).

ARCHITECTURE

CHAPTER 2

A Tibetan Architecture?
The Traditional Buildings of Lo

John Harrison

The earliest known dwellings in Lo are not buildings, but caves, networks of tunnels, multistorey villages chiselled into the soft conglomerate cliffs of the river canyons bisecting this high mountain desert (figure 2.1). The great Kali Gandaki cuts south through the main Himalayan chain between the 8,000-metre peaks of Dhaulagiri and Annapurna, creating a route which for centuries and millennia has carried peoples and trade and religions between the Tibetan plateau and Nepal and the Indian plains. It was also a road for invading armies and marauding tribes, so the inaccessible cave villages provided a place of refuge for their inhabitants as well as a retreat from the harsh winters and constant winds.

Archaeological investigation of cave systems in the Muktinath Valley of southern Lo has dated their occupation as far back as 1200 BCE,[1] but as yet very little is known of these early inhabitants of Lo. They were probably of Tibeto-Burman stock, and remained in the area as later Tibetan migrants arrived. While keeping the cave systems in occupation they also began to build compact multistorey clusters of houses at the base of the cliffs, almost as if they were trying to replicate the cave-like character of their earlier dwellings. At the archaeological sites studied, both caves and houses were abandoned by the end of the 16th century as villages grew around the new Tibetan castles. However, in Tsoshar (or Choshar), northeast of Lo Möntang, caves and houses together continue in use today.

This pre-Tibetan form of village building persisted after the Tibetanization of Lo, particularly in Shöyül, the area immediately south of Upper Lo, where even the original language, Seke, is still spoken.[2]

The village of Te (Tetang in Nepali) appears as a single massive structure, sheer walls of rammed earth rising through five or six storeys and presenting a continuous blank defensive perimeter to the outside (figure 2.2). Individual houses have often only one room on each floor, connected by steep wooden ladders gradually rising from the darkness to the flat roof bounded by stacks of firewood. These houses have almost no decoration, no stylistic details to link them to Tibet except the bracketed heads to the doors and tiny windows. Indeed this strong, simple architecture developed in the Himalaya before Tibet existed, but it then became one of the elements from which Tibetan architecture was created.

TIBETAN EMPIRE

The influence of Tibet was first felt in the Lo area with the westward expansion of the Yarlung empire in the 7th century, when Tibetan armies penetrated as far south as Lower Lo. Buddhist missionaries were also active, so it is probable that some Tibetan religious buildings were erected. Padmasambhava, the Indian tantric guru, is said to have founded Lo Gekar monastery in the mid-8th century before travelling on to Lhasa and

2.1 Yara, northeast Lo. Cave settlement in eroded cliffs.

2.2 Te village. High rammed-earth walls and multistorey houses.

establishing Samyè monastery in 779. The massive walls at the core of Lo Gekar may date from this early period, but much of the building is later. In fact, for several hundred years, through the collapse of the Tibetan empire after 842 and the rise of various Western Tibetan states, and then the resurgence of Buddhism in the 10th century, there is not much clear evidence for the architectural activity that was certainly taking place in Lo. Many renowned religious figures, including Rinchen Zangpo (958–1055) and Milarepa (1040–1123), passed through, and in their histories there are references to the monasteries, now lost, where they stayed. Throughout Lo one finds eroded fragments of massive earth walls, traces of unknown castles and monasteries. It can only be assumed that Tibetan culture, through

Buddhist teaching and practice, and through the neighbouring secular powers of Western Tibet, had a continuing and growing impact in Lo.

The cave temple at Luri, once part of a much larger cave monastery, may date from the early 14th century. Its exquisite paintings and stupa show that there were sponsors rich and powerful enough to attract artists of the highest quality (see chapter 5). But no major monuments remain from this period, until suddenly, in the 15th century, the Lo dynasty burst into political activity and artistic creativity. And because the lineage of the Lo kings has remarkably continued until today, their history and their monuments have also survived.

THE KINGDOM OF LO

Amapel (1388–1447) established the new kingdom of Lo in 1440, although his father and grandfather, military rulers of Gungtang's western territories, had already enjoyed virtual independence for half a century.[3] On the "Plain of Aspiration" below earlier hilltop forts, several hours north of his existing seat at Tsarang, he immediately built a new capital, Lo Möntang, surrounded by square walls and towers (figure 2.3). Inside the walls was a four-storey palace and Jampa Lhakhang (Maitreya temple), a vast temple taller than the palace (figure 2.4). Twenty-five years later a second large temple, Tupchen Lhakhang (Mahamuni temple), was built, as well as rows of stupas. Both temples were fully decorated with wall paintings which are among the finest examples of Tibetan art of this period (see chapters 6, 8, and 9). The scale and imagination of this enterprise suggest a considerable degree of sophistication on the part of Amapel and his son Agön Zangpo who ascended the throne in 1447, and an appreciation of contemporary developments in Tibetan art and architecture. Lo was intended to be a centre of Tibetan culture as well as a base for the new kingdom's territorial expansion.

The square plan and the walls and towers of the town may be traced back ultimately to the ideal cities of the Chinese, but perhaps more immediately to the defensive walls of the Gungtang capital Dzongkha and those of Sakya monastery.[4] The Sakyapa school dominated Buddhist teaching in Lo by this time, and Ngorchen Künga Zangpo, founder of Ngor Sakya monastery, came to Lo three times as spiritual adviser to Amapel and Agön. He was present in Lo from 1447 to 1449 for the construction and consecration of Jampa Lhakhang, and it might be surmised that he had also been involved in the foundation of the temple and the new town.

The painted mandalas of Jampa Lhakhang are the treasures of Lo, but the building itself is an important example of Tibetan architecture. The red tower still dominates the little town and the surrounding landscape, but the temple has seen significant alterations during its history. Originally the tower was of two storeys. The third floor was added in 1498 (figure 2.5), and in 1663 the present two-storey-high Maitreya statue on its massive base was inserted by cutting back the first-floor structure.[5] The present entrance courtyard was most likely the assembly hall, Dukhang, with a complete roof

2.3 Chödé monastery, Lo Möntang. Carved mani stones in front of the painted city wall around the monastery.

2.4 Jampa Lhakhang, Lo Möntang, 1447. View from the east, 1993, before restoration by the American Himalayan Foundation.

2.5 Jampa Lhakhang. Section showing the massive earth walls and finely carved woodwork within.

2.6 Jampa Lhakhang. Wooden capital in the courtyard with scrolls and carved Sanskrit inscription.

supported by a regular grid of columns, and ancillary accommodation on an upper floor. This temple form, of assembly hall and inner chapel surrounded on three sides and three levels by circumambulatory passages, is very similar to the Gyantsé Penkhor Chödé completed in 1425.

Tupchen Lhakhang was originally a single large hall, entered from the east. It was lit by a central raised lantern, its high ceiling supported by seven rows of six columns. Later alterations have included the addition of an entrance vestibule containing four large guardian sculptures, the rebuilding of the north wall one bay inwards, and the loss of two floors of accommodation on the roof. The change to the north wall has also affected the sculptures on their platform against the west wall, where a fourth later figure of Guru Rinpoché has been added in the northwest corner, perhaps replacing a stupa which matched that in the southwest corner. There has also been some interchange of elements between Tupchen and Jampa Lhakhang, as capitals from Jampa (surplus from a Dukhang/courtyard re-ordering?) are found in Tupchen, and Tupchen capitals and pillars (from the lost northern row?) are reused in the Jampa courtyard.

The designs of the two sets of capitals are quite distinct. Tupchen has the long arms and cloud motifs, elegantly carved, typical of central and southwest Tibet, whereas Jampa has a more triangular design with varying numbers of scrolls (figure 2.6). In the courtyard and middle floor these are carved with Sanskrit prayers on one side and a dragon face on the other. On the lower floor of the sanctum the scroll capitals are cruciform in plan, with four arms supporting a coffered ceiling of square bays. These scroll designs are unusual for Central Tibetan architecture, but scrolls, albeit of rather different designs, appear in early Ladakhi temples such as at Alchi, and in Western Tibet at Tsaparang. They may be traced back westwards to the Ionic volutes of Hellenistic architecture which flourished in Bactria and Gandhara (e.g. the Zoroastrian temple at Jaulian, Taxila, 1st century BCE).[6]

The art and architecture of the Lo dynasty was formed by Gungtang, Sakya, Gyantsé, and Central Tibet to the east, but there were also cultural influences from the west. Lo's history is a continuing story of conflict and concord with western neighbours, with Gugé-Purang north of the Himalaya, Ladakh further west, and with western Nepal – first as the Khasa-Yatse kingdom and then as Jumla. All these states fell within the sphere of Tibetan culture[7] and were to some extent inheritors of the Tibetan empire, so they had much in common. Surprisingly little architectural influence came from the south. Lo grew rich on the busy north-south trade through the Kali Gandaki, and Newar art had flowered at Luri a century before Lo Möntang was built and decorated, but there is no sign that the singular architecture of the Kathmandu Valley travelled north.

TIBETAN ARCHITECTURE IN LO

It was suggested earlier that pre-Tibetan, pre-Buddhist architectural elements survived, subsumed in the new Tibetan architecture. Indigenous and Tibetan architectures held in common the available building materials – earth, stone, timber – and basic construction techniques – masonry walls and timber floors – but the scale of operation and the degree of elaboration were entirely different. Archaeological investigations of early settlement sites in southern Mustang such as Khyingga in the Muktinath Valley, and Garap Dzong (on the left bank of the Kali Gandaki, opposite Jomsom, the capital of the short-

2.7 Tupchen Lhakhang. Interior, perspective section through the central lantern showing the possible original disposition of the statuary at the western end in 1472.

lived little kingdom of Sum in the 16th century, have found indications that some structures were more important than the ordinary dwellings, but there is nothing like the vast temples which the kings of Lo were building further north.

We can take Tupchen Lhakhang as a particularly clear example of Tibetan construction: four walls and a flat roof supported by beams and pillars. The massive walls are rammed-earth on a stone base, 5 feet/1.5 metres thick and 22 feet/6.7 metres high to the ceiling. Seven beams span from north to south, each supported by six pillars (figure 2.7). The six central bays of the roof are raised to form a lantern 27 feet/8.2 metres high, supported by two taller pillars. The pillars are a composite construction, not single tree-trunks, but separate boards and sections fitted and dovetailed together, an ingenious solution for a shortage of large trees. In contrast, Jampa Lhakhang does have pillars of massive round tree-trunks, but cut into sections and stacked vertically, presumably to facilitate transport from the forests far to the south. The Tupchen capitals are of the most common Central and southwest Tibetan design, finely executed and painted with gilded Sanskrit mantras. Above the main beams, painted with gilded dragons, are the three standard Tibetan mouldings of lotus leaf, tiny cubes, and discs, and then two superimposed rows of projecting brackets, the

2.8 Royal palace, Lo Möntang, 1441. Typical Tibetan cloud-motif capital.

square-section roof joists, and the ceiling of willow sticks. In the central lantern the projecting brackets are replaced by carved lions, a motif from India and Gandhara which first appeared in Tibetan architecture in the Lhasa Jokhang, but which subsequently was also widely employed in early Western Tibetan architecture.

The creation of these superlative examples of Tibetan architecture and painting came at the early peak of the Lo kingdom's power and wealth. Nothing produced subsequently in Lo can be compared to them, but they provided a template for future building throughout Lo and the wider area of Tibetan Buddhist influence. For a century Lo flourished, and to promote the kingdom as an important religious centre royal patrons built stupas, mani walls (of stone tablets with the inscription "om mani padme hum"), and temples and refurbished the major monasteries of Tsarang, Namgyel, and Gemi as well as Jampa and Tupchen. When village temples were rebuilt or extended they looked to mainstream Tibetan models for their planning and their decoration, although there are many untutored local variations to be seen. Secular architecture – palaces, and then houses – was equally affected by Tibetan norms. In the now-empty lower floors of the royal palace in Lo

2.9 Tangye, a remote village in eastern Lo. The stupas built for the gods occupy almost as much land as the village houses.

2.10 Monumental stupa protecting the road into Tsarang. A flat roof on wooden posts shelters the plastered mud brick dome.

Möntang, for instance, the first building in the new town in 1441, there are finely carved capitals with the cloud-motif design (figure 2.8).

But from the mid-16th century Jumla became the dominant regional power, controlling trade and reducing Lo at times to a small area around its capital. Building was much curtailed, although alliances with Ladakh afforded some respite from Jumla's incursions. Chödé monastery in Lo Möntang was built in 1710, and the city walls extended to enclose it, and further south Kutsap Ternga monastery, and the impressive Gönpa Khang opposite Tsuk (Chusang). When independent principalities in southern Lo were established in the 16th century by nobles from Lo Möntang, new castles and temples were built in Kak (Kagbeni), Dzar, and Dzong (a hamlet on the right bank of the Muktinath river, opposite Dzar).

Lo remained a Tibetan landscape. The most prominent signs of man's inhabitation are still the castles and palaces of the aristocracy, the red-painted Buddhist monasteries, and monumental domed stupas[8] marking roads and villages (figures 2.9 and 2.10).

LO AND NEPAL

Lo retained a considerable degree of autonomy when the Gorkhas defeated Jumla and unified Nepal in 1789, but suffered setbacks in the mid-19th century when the crucial north-south trade through the Kali Gandaki was monopolized by the Thakalis further south. Tukché became the principal entrepot, the interchange for caravans from India and Tibet, and a new architecture of grand trading houses and caravanserais developed there. Two-storey houses were built around generous courtyards, with timber arcades below and large richly-decorated windows above. The detailing was a fusion of Tibetan motifs and Newar woodwork from the Kathmandu Valley, although the building form, with thick masonry walls and flat roofs, was still essentially Tibetan. The courtyard house is well-adapted to the Lo climate, trapping the winter sun and providing domestic space sheltered from the strong winds of the Kali Gandaki Valley.

As the Thakali economic, political, and social influences spread northwards, so did its architecture (figure 2.11). This is particularly evident in Baragaon, southern Lo, where the new architectural style can be seen in a number of large houses built in the late 19th and early 20th centuries, but it also found its way as far north as Lo Möntang.

* * *

In 1950–51 China occupied Tibet, and from 1959 the border was closed, so that Lo lost both its northern trade and its historic cultural links with Tibet. But interestingly, in recent years the major schools of Tibetan Buddhism have had an increasing influence from their exile bases in India, as newly-trained lamas return to Lo to revive local institutions and build new temples.

As communications within Nepal improved in the second half of the 20th century, and as Kathmandu extended local government and education systems to the remote corners of the country, the influence of the metropolitan centre began to be felt in many ways: new offices, new schools, new hospitals; and often new materials, imported cement and tin sheets, however inappropriate in this climate and landscape. Tourism, too, had a considerable impact, first in the 1970s along the Annapurna trekking route, and then with the limited opening of Upper Lo from 1992 (figure 2.12). New building types, lodges and hotels, developed from the local tea-houses catering for travellers, and provincial visitors to Kathmandu brought back the latest fashions, in building as well as in clothes.

The vernacular architecture of Lo is already under pressure, and this will increase when the new road from the south to Lo Möntang, now under construction, finally links up. Traditional building has never been static, and has always, as we have seen, gradually assimilated new influences, but if change is too rapid then the positive features of traditional building may be lost in the rush for development and improvement. The monuments will survive, preserved for posterity,[9] but they should be seen in the environment from which they grew.

2.11 Dzar, southern Lo. Courtyard of a 19th-century house with timber arcades and large windows in Thakali style showing the influence of Newar carving from the Kathmandu Valley.

2.12 Rasta and reggae on the Annapurna circuit: Hotel Bob Marley, a trekking lodge in Muktinath, 2005.

FIGURE ACKNOWLEDGEMENTS

All photographs and drawings by John Harrison.

NOTES

1   At the earliest dates, the caves investigated were in use as cemeteries. A. Simons and W. Schon, "Cave systems and terrace settlements in Mustang, Nepal: Settlement periods from prehistoric times up to the present day", *Beitrage zur Allgemeinen und Vergleichenden Archaologie*, band 18, 1998, pp. 27–47.

2   C. Ramble and C. Sceber. "Dead and living settlements in the Shoyul of Mustang", *Ancient Nepal*, 138, 1995, pp. 107–30.

3   R.K. Dhungel, *The Kingdom of Lo (Mustang): A Historical Study*, Kathmandu, 2002, pp. 75ff.

4   J. Harrison, "Kings' castles and sacred squares: the founding of Lo Monthang", *Sacred Landscape of the Himalaya*, ed. N. Gutschow et al., Vienna, 2003, pp. 55–66.

5   A hypothesis based on an examination of the structure with Roberto Vitali and Robert Powell in 1993. R. Vitali, "On Byams pa and Thub chen lha khang of Glo sMos thang", *Tibet Journal*, 24/1, 1996, pp. 3–28.

6   P. Mortari Vergara, "Tibet Occidental (Ngari) du Xeme au XIVeme siecle", *Demeures des hommes, sanctuaires des dieux,* ed. P. Mortari Vergara and G. Béguin, Rome, 1987, pp. 286, 295.

7   Although by the 17th century Jumla was completely Hinduized. L. Petech, "Ya-t'se, Gu-ge, Pu-raṇ: a new study", *Selected Papers on Asian History*, Rome, 1988, p. 382.

8   The flat roof and posts protecting the earth brick domes are distinctive features of stupas in Lo and neighbouring Nyeshang and Dölpo, and Limi further west. Elsewhere in the Tibetan world roofed stupas are only found in Kham, far to the east.

9   The American Himalayan Foundation and architects John Sanday Associates have been engaged for the last decade in a splendid restoration of Lo's historic buildings, training craftsmen and encouraging the involvement of local people in the future of their heritage.

PAINTING AND SCULPTURE

CHAPTER 3

Cave Hermitages and Chapels
in Eastern Lo

Erberto Lo Bue

aves have been excavated in the conglomerate cliffs of Lo since prehistoric times, as shown by John Harrison in his contribution to this volume (see figure 2.1), and are a feature of much of its landscape. Some were used as funerary chambers, others as dwellings, granaries, and even jails. In the 1960s caves sheltered Tibetan fighters during their guerrilla warfare against the Chinese army, which had invaded Tibet during the previous decade.[1] Some were reoccupied by local people following devastating floods in the 1990s and some are still inhabited today, for example at the village of Mahrang.[2] That does not appear so surprising, if one considers that the cave dwellings in the city of Matera, in southern Italy, were abandoned only about half a century ago.[3]

The spread of various Buddhist schools in Lo led to the excavation of temples, hermitages, and monastic dwellings, just as had been the case in India and Central Asia from ancient times. The walls of cave temples were occasionally carved with images,[4] but more often they were painted with murals, some of which have survived to this day, particularly in the eastern part of the country. All cave hermitages and monastic dwellings, like most of their temples, were abandoned in due course because of changed historical and geological factors, erosion having made access to them difficult, if not impossible. However, a few chapels still function: for instance, one at the cave hermitage of Mentsi, about a kilometre east of Tsuk (or Chusang), in Lower Lo. Like other caves in Lo, this hermitage is traditionally related to Padmasambhava, though it was established in 1003 by a lama, Künzang Logyel,[5] apparently with the help of religious people from Manang as well as local people, and was abandoned around 1864. Its main chapel is surrounded by a circumambulation corridor in conformity with the traditional Indian Buddhist architectural pattern found also in the much earlier cave temples of the Deccan.

Its main image, in spite of being regarded by villagers as the bodhisattva and future Buddha Maitreya, actually represents the cosmic Buddha Vairochana[6] and is placed on the ledge protruding from the main wall of the chapel. More clay images, portraying the bodhisattva Avalokiteshvara and the other cosmic Buddhas, Amoghasiddhi being represented twice, are placed on the ledges along the side walls. The wall supporting Vairochana encases a damaged stone panel in Indo-Newar style[7] carved with the goddess Tara (figure 3.1), which has been attributed to the 8th century, though it is more likely to have been fashioned by the Newar artists that Künzang Logyel summoned from the Nepal Valley when he founded the hermitage in the very early 11th century.[8] The image of the goddess is flanked by vertical registers carved with standing figures, the whole composition being surrounded by frames decorated with vegetable scrolls that are ultimately of Hellenistic origin. What is left of the murals on

3.1 Tara. Mentsi hermitage, Tsuk, 11th century. Stone. Photograph: Amy Heller.

the same wall, some illustrating episodes from Shakyamuni's life (figure 3.2), has been tentatively attributed to the 12th century,[9] though it might date to the foundation of the hermitage.

To the second half of the following century might belong the wall paintings extant in two chapels at different cave hermitages belonging to a group of four: one among the scattered ruins and caves of the monastic centre of Könchokling ("Island of the Most Precious Ones" with reference to the three jewels of Buddhism: the Buddha, the dharma, and the monastic community), northeast of Möntang and about an hour's ride from the Tibetan border; the other, known as Rindzinling ("Island of the Possessors of Knowledge"), in the northeast area of Tsoshar (or Choshar). Due to progressive erosion and increasing difficulty of access, both hermitages have been abandoned for a couple of centuries, a ladder being necessary to reach up the entrance to the latter, opening in a cliff, whereas access to the former

3.2 Siddhartha in an archery contest. Mentsi cave temple, Tsuk, 11th–12th century. Distemper. Photograph: Chiara Bellini.

requires a rope to reach down a narrow path leading to its partly collapsed twin chapel cave.[10]

Three cycles of paintings in the cave hermitage of Könchokling are discussed by Luigi Fieni in Chapter 4. From a stylistic point of view, even though they were eventually interpreted as upper corners of a curtain hanging behind the throne, the stylized triangular flames above the shoulders of some figures in the chapel devoted to the primordial Buddha Vajradhara (see figure 4.1) are found in the art of Gandhara and characterize also the Indo-Newar style predominating in Tibetan painting until the 15th century, even more so in Lo, as shown by a detail illustrated by Fieni in his contribution on the temple of Maitreya (see figure 8.12).

The disposition of figures in registers in the chapel devoted to tantric masters is also typical of the Indo-Newar aesthetics as found both in murals in the Nepal Valley, for example in the ancient royal palace of Kathmandu, and in the long horizontal cotton paintings known by Newars as *vilampo* (scroll painting). The division in panels of the various scenes portraying the siddhas with their attendants is sometimes underlined by the presence of trees, occasionally separating figures within the same composition. An echo of this kind of arrangement is found in a Sakya cultural context in the famous 15th-century murals depicting the mahasiddhas in the Chapel of the Path and Fruit in the main monastic building at Gyantsé, in southwest Tibet, where the border-lines of registers and panels have disappeared, leaving the role of separating the various figures exclusively to vegetable elements – flowers or trees.[11]

The liveliness of the portraits of tantric masters, painted with a very limited palette and hardly any background decoration, foreshadows that of some drawings found in a famous 15th-century Newar sketchbook preserved in the Neotia Collection in Varanasi.[12] The drawing of a penis ejaculating at the back of the mahasiddha's female attendant illustrated in Fieni's relevant contribution (see figure 4.6) is reminiscent of those painted on the outer walls of Bhutanese farmhouses to distract and ward off evil spirits, though they are also symbols of fertility.[13] The lines in the inscriptions under the panels allow us to identify the main figures in the composition, the guru Tambaka in the case of the siddha with the female attendant mentioned above, described in devotional verses drawn from a prayer written by an abbot of Bodhgaya, and edited and translated into Tibetan in the 1150s or 1160s.[14] It should be mentioned also that during the spring of the Newar year 251, corresponding to 1131 CE, an iconographic text on the 84 siddhas had been completed in the Nepal Valley by the monk Shrisena, apparently a Newar scholar.[15]

The baggy garments with wide folds worn by masters portrayed on the walls in the chapel devoted to the Buddha Vajradhara are stylistically reminiscent of those found in some portraits of Kagyü masters, for example in the Temple of the Translator at the famous site of Alchi, in Ladakh, or the Temple of the Guru at the foot of the ruins of the castle of Piyang, in central Ladakh,[16] with which the iconographic programme in the hermitage of Könchokling seems to share a non-sectarian attitude.

Rindzinling was excavated in a cliff at an altitude of 4,291 metres and was possibly related to the Kagyü order of the monastery of Drigung, in Central Tibet, which was particularly active in Western Tibet as well as in Ladakh from the 13th century onwards, for instance at Alchi, and whose influence was felt in Lo, too.[17] Indeed it may be suggested that the ascetic trend characterizing the early Kagyü tradition, as represented by the famous mystic and poet Milarepa in Tibet, is reflected by several cave hermitages in Lo, as opposed to the built-up monasteries and hermitages generally belonging to the Sakya, Nyingma, and Bön traditions.

As indicated by its inscription, a detail on the lower southern section of the west wall in the best-preserved chapel of this hermitage (figure 3.3), depicts a famous 7th-century statue of Arya Lokeshvara (Avalokiteshvara) known as "Pakpa Wati", "Jowo Wati", "Kyirong Jowo", or simply "Jowo", wearing Newar garments and housed at the temple of Kyirong in southwest Tibet and not far from the Nepal border, until 1959.[18] Tibetan historiography places it in a group of four sandalwood "brother" images, one of which was set up at Bungamati, in the Nepal Valley, by King Narendradeva, who started a famous chariot festival devoted to that bodhisattva still performed today.[19] The Nepalese ruler is credited with having initiated – during his long exile in Tibet – his host, the Tibetan emperor Songtsen Gampo, to the cult of Avalokiteshvara. This bodhisattva is believed to have created the Tibetan people by taking the form of a monkey and mating with a demoness of the rocks. Songtsen Gampo and, later, the Dalai Lamas came to be regarded as manifestations of Avalokiteshvara. According to Tibetan tradition, the Kyirong Lokeshvara was the first Buddhist image brought to Tibet from the Nepal Valley, the second being the statue of Arya Lokeshvara preserved in the Dalai Lamas' palace built near Lhasa on the hill that was thereafter called Potala after the name of the mountain upon which that bodhisattva is supposed to dwell in India. A copy of the second statue is illustrated in the historical introduction to this volume (see figure 1.2).

The temple housing the statue of Avalokiteshvara at Kyirong is the only important construction in Tibet built in the pagoda style typical of Nepalese architecture, characterizing accordingly the religious buildings painted on the adjacent southern wall, west of the window in the chapel of Rindzinling. Inscriptions on the same wall refer also to the Nepalese queen who took that image as a dowry to Songtsen Gampo and who had the Trülnang built in Lhasa in order to house the more famous Jowo, the statue of the Buddha[20] brought by the Chinese consort of the same emperor, after which the Trülnang came to be commonly known as "Jokhang". According to a Tibetan source, the Jowo Wati statue brought along by the Nepalese princess and kept at Kyirong had a red complexion (obviously the colour of the sandalwood out of which it was made), one face, and two hands, the right one making the boon-bestowing gesture and the other holding a lotus,[21] a description corresponding to the depiction of the statue in this chapel.

3.3 The Jowo Lokeshvara of Kyirong. Rindzinling cave temple, 13th century. Distemper. Photograph: Chiara Bellini.

The temple of Kyirong was one of the most famous and important ones in the area controlled by the rulers of Gungtang. Atisha spent a year there in 1045 and the temple was also visited by important masters belonging to different Kagyü religious orders from the 12th to the 14th century, as well as by the Indian scholar Vanaratna in the 15th century.[22] Two of its most illustrious visitors were the famous scholar Sakya Panchen (1182–1251) and his nephew and successor, Pakpa, who established the supremacy of the monastery of Sakya in Tibet. That visit is even illustrated on the southern wall of the Temple of the Path and Fruit in the main monastic building at Gyantsé.[23] The image of Arya Lokeshvara also received a visit by the Lo scholar Sönam Lhündrup (1456–1532), who wrote a eulogy as well as a history of the statue.[24]

A damaged mandala painted below a register depicting the five cosmic Buddhas on the southern wall east of the window in the same chapel is reminiscent of other mandalas painted in cave temples of Lo and of some of those found in temples at Alchi. The rare iconography of an 18-armed Garuda on the wall showing the religious buildings mentioned above is also found in a more sophisticated image painted in the 15th-century Temple of the Guru at Piyang, a reminder of the pervasive Kagyü influence in Western and southwest Tibet, Ladakh, as well as Lo from the 13th century.[25] The paintings on the other walls include historical figures such as Padmasambhava, who plays a particularly prominent role in both Nyingma and Kagyü religious traditions and iconography, as well as a stupa related perhaps to a Kagyü master. From a stylistic point of view one may notice, above the shoulders of some figures, the stylized triangular flames already mentioned in relation to some images at Könchokling, as well as the depiction of trees with their foliage in the shape of balloons, as in 14th-century murals in the monastery of Zhalu.

To the same cultural environment, period, and style may be related the mandalas painted on the walls and ceiling of another cave hermitage, located west of Rindzinling at a site known as Nupchokling, at an altitude of 4,018 metres (figure 3.4), and belonging to the group of four hermitages including Könchokling and Rindzinling.

The stupa cave temple of Trashi Geling, dated to the late 13th or early 14th century (figure 3.5),[26] was excavated along steep cliffs above the Yara river, a left side tributary of the Kali Gandaki, like that of Luri discussed by Helmut and Heidi Neumann in chapter 5. Stupa cave temples

Below
3.4 Mandalas. Nupchok cave temple, 13th century. Distemper. Photograph: Luigi Fieni.

Opposite
3.5 Stupa. Trashi Geling cave temple, 13th–14th century. Photograph: Luigi Fieni.

in Lo, ultimately related to the much earlier and larger examples in the
Deccan, were the object of veneration as long as they were accessible,
until at least half a century ago.[27] The walls in the Trashi Geling cave
temple are painted with the six-syllable invocation "om mani padme hum",
traditionally associated with Avalokiteshvara in his four-armed manifestation
as Shadakshara ("Six Syllables") Lokeshvara and personified by the goddess
Shadakshari Mahavidya ("The Great Science of the Six Syllables").[28] Next to
Shadakshara Lokeshvara there is the portrait of a lama wearing a robe with a
prominent armhole of the type found particularly in some portraits of Kagyü
masters during the 13th and 14th centuries (figure 3.6). The lower margin of
the mural is delimited by a geometrical lozenge pattern originally indicating
the billows of samsara (cycle of birth, death, and rebirth) and found in
murals of Western Tibet and Ladakh, for example at Alchi or in the Temple
of the Guru at Piyang.

3.6 Shadakshara Lokeshvara with a lama.
Trashi Geling cave temple, 13th–14th
century. Photograph: Luigi Fieni.

On the whole, the style of the wall paintings in this hermitage reflects
the Newar version of Indian aesthetics as found for instance in the finest
murals painted during the first half of the 14th century in the Golden
Temple of the monastery of Zhalu, in southwest Tibet. Indeed it is likely
that the murals in the stupa cave temple of Trashi Geling, like those painted
in the Mentsi hermitage mentioned above, were painted by artists from the
Nepal Valley, who have been active in Lo throughout its history,[29] as proved
by the inscriptions reporting the names of Newar painters and sculptors in
temples, and of silversmiths on artefacts, in Möntang, and referred to in
various chapters of this volume.[30]

To the late 14th or early 15th century may belong the paintings in
the cave hermitage of Chödzong ("Dharma Castle"),[31] which is related to
the Kagyü and Nyingma traditions. The hermitage, facing south, lies east
of Könchokling, roughly on the same latitude as Möntang. It was partly
excavated and partly built on the cliffs rising above a settlement, now in
ruins, along the right bank of the Yarsang stream, which runs from northeast
to southwest and is crossed by a path leading to Tibet through the Chak pass
(4,000 m). The extension of the ruins suggests that this village must have
profited not only from its nearby pastures, but also from trade with Tibet.

According to its keeper, the hermitage of Chödzong is a Kagyü
and Nyingma (Kanying) institution, as implied also by the composite
iconography of the mediocre and partly damaged 19th–20th-century
murals in the assembly hall, depicting Kagyü religious masters as well as
Padmasambhava, Samantabhadra as a Buddha, and other typically Nyingma
cycles. However, some of the portraits painted in the vault of the cave
temple behind the assembly hall suggest a Sakya affiliation, too, hence the
non-sectarian tradition of this foundation, which was presumably used by
practitioners belonging to different schools. The murals in the cave temple
at Chödzong share some features with the Temple of the Guru at Piyang, in
particular the occasional shading in the complexion of the main images and
a sketchy quality in the drawings of minor figures, as well as a composite
iconographic programme with Kagyü, Sakya, and Nyingma features.

Opposite
3.7 Chödzong cave temple, 14th–15th
century. Photograph: Luigi Fieni.

Pages 50–51
3.8 Yamantaka. Chödzong cave temple,
14th–15th century. Distemper. Photograph:
Luigi Fieni.
3.9 Vajrabhairava. Chödzong cave temple,
14th–15th century. Distemper. Photograph:
Luigi Fieni.

The hermitage houses metal images, including the portrait of a presumably Kagyü lama, which were rescued from a ruined cave temple in the area, as well as clay statues of protectors of the dharma, in the square chapel excavated behind the assembly hall (figure 3.7). The most interesting feature of the chapel, which can be reached through a very short and low passage, is provided by the murals surviving on the walls and vault, in spite of the fact that many paintings have disappeared. They represent several important tantric tutelary deities of Buddha rank embracing their consorts within their realms, with the lamas who transmitted their tantric cycles portrayed in the registers above and their attendant deities painted in the registers below (figures 3.8–3.13). They are identified by inscriptions which, despite several spelling mistakes, bear also the names of at least eight donors, both religious masters and aristocrats, including a couple of female ones.

3.10 Guhyasamaja. Chödzong cave temple, 14th–15th century. Distemper. Photograph: Luigi Fieni.

3.11 Vajrasattva. Chödzong cave temple, 14th–15th century. Distemper. Photograph: Luigi Fieni.

3.12 Kalachakra. Chödzong cave temple,
14th–15th century. Distemper. Photograph:
Luigi Fieni.

3.13 Hevajra. Chödzong cave temple,
14th–15th century. Distemper. Photograph:
Luigi Fieni.

Proceeding clockwise as one enters the cave there are Yamantaka (figure 3.8) and Vajrabhairava (figure 3.9) – two deities that are often confused in spite of the presence of inscriptions – Guhyasamaja (figure 3.10), Vajrasattva as a Buddha (figure 3.11), Kalachakra (figure 3.12), Hevajra (figure 3.13), and so forth. Niches with trilobate arches surround the two tutelary deities having peaceful expressions (figures 3.10 and 3.11), while those with a fierce mien are surrounded by mandorlas of flames (figures 3.8, 3.9, 3.12, and 3.13). This hermitage, one of the very few that has not been abandoned altogether, bears witness to an important non-sectarian religious, cultural, and artistic period in the history of Lo, preceding the foundation of larger, built-up monastic institutions under the influence of the prince abbots of Sakya.

NOTES

1   M. Shepherd Slusser and L.M. Bishop, "Another Luri: A Newly Discovered Cave *Chorten* in Mustang, Nepal", *Orientations*, 30/2, February 1999, p. 18.

2   Cf. R.K. Dhungel, *The Kingdom of Lo (Mustang): A Historical Study*, Kathmandu, 2002, p. 306.

3   Those caves were included in the UNESCO World Heritage list in 1993.

4   Cf. G. Tucci, *Tra giungle e pagode*, Roma, 1979, fig. 41 between pp. 64 and 65.

5   Harsha Muni Shakya, "The Contributions of Shakya Bhikshu Ruptejpal in the Development of the Kingdom of Blo", *Pragati*, 2/1, January 2004.

6   Cf. D. Snellgrove, *Himalayan Pilgrimage*, Boulder, 1981, p. 171. A similar confusion has occurred at the monastery of Tabo, where a statue of Vairochana mistaken for an image of the cosmic Buddha Amitabha is painted red. Snellgrove translates the name Mentsi as "Medicinal Juice" (*sMan rtsi*).

7   In the context of Tibetan aesthetics, the issue of Newar vs. Indian idiom is largely artificial, since the Newar style was perceived as an Indian sub-style even by such an eminent Tibetan scholar and connoisseur as Pemakarpo in the 16th century.

8   Cf. Shakya. Its style is quite dissimilar, for instance, to that of the 8th-century Tara from Sarnath kept at the National Museum in New Delhi. Cf. P. Pal, *The Arts of Nepal*, Part I, *Sculpture*, Leiden/Köln, 1974, pl. 219.

9   Cf. Slusser and Bishop, p. 20, fig. 6.

10   According to its keeper, the cave monastery of Könchokling was accessible until two centuries ago, before erosion destroyed or made very awkward the access to it.

11   A similar device is used also in Byzantine mosaics, for example at Ravenna, in Italy.

12   Cf. J. Lowry, "A Fifteenth Century Sketchbook (Preliminary Study)", *Essais sur l'art du Tibet*, ed. A. Macdonald and Y. Imaeda, Paris, 1977.

13   Cf. H. Richardson, "Phallic Symbols in Tibet", *Bulletin of Tibetology*, IX/2, 1972, p. 25; and M. Dujardin, "From Fortress to Farmhouse: A Living Architecture", *Bhutan: Mountain Fortress of the Gods*, ed. C. Schicklgruber and F. Pommaret, London/ Vienna, 1997, p. 75. Though apparently associated with Drukpa Künlé (1455–1529), a famous "mad" yogin and poet of the Kagyü tradition, their iconography is much earlier and most probably pre-Buddhist.

14   Cf. A. Egyed, *The Eighty-four Siddhas: A Tibetan Blockprint from Mongolia*, Budapest, 1984, pp. 12–13 and 99, with R. Linrothe, *Holy Madness: Portraits of Tantric Siddhas*, Chicago, 2006, p. 429, n. 42. A brahman by caste, Tambaka became a coppersmith and obtained the siddhi (accomplishment) of swiftfootedness.

15   Cf. the colophon translated by P. Cordier, *Catalogue du Fonds Tibétain de la Bibliotèque Nationale. Index du Bstan-ḥgyur*, Part III, Paris, 1915, p. 475, CXXIII/8, and published as well as translated by T. Schmid, *The Eighty-five Siddhas*, Stockholm, 1958, p. 169, providing this date, which is different from the one reported by D. Martin in Linrothe, p. 122.

16   Cf. "The Gu ru lha khang at Phyi dbang: a Mid-15th Century Temple in Central Ladakh", *Discoveries in Western Tibet and the Himalayas: Essays on History, Literature,*

Archaeology and Art: PIATS 2003, Vol. 10/8, ed. A. Heller and G. Orofino, Leiden/ Boston, 2007, pp. 175–96.

17 Cf. J. Kramer, *A Noble Abbot from Mustang: Life and Works of Glo-bo mKhan-chen (1456–1532)*, Wien, 2008, pp. 14–15.

18 On this image see F.-K. Ehrhard, *Die Statue und der Tempel des Órya Va-ti bzang-po: Ein Beitrag zu Geschichte und Geographie des tibetischen Buddhismus*, Wiesbaden, 2004. Cf. T. Wylie, *A Tibetan Religious Geography of Nepal,* Roma, 1970, pp. 14–15, n. 20; and Yang Shuwen et al., *Buddhist Thang-ka Art of Tibet: The Biographical Paintings of 'Phags pa*, Beijing/Lhasa, 1987, p. 152, No. 23-2. This statue seems to be confused by Western translators with the more famous Jowo of Lhasa. The epithet Jowo ("Lord") is applied by Tibetans to particularly famous historical figures and images.

19 On the history of these four images cf. Sönam Gyeltsen's *The Mirror Illuminating the Royal Genealogies*, ed. P. Sørensen, Wiesbaden, 1994, pp. 194–95, with I. Alsop, "Phagpa Lokeśvara of the Potala", *Orientations*, 21/4, April 1999, pp. 58–60.

20 *'Phrul snang* and *Jo bo Shag kya* (namely the Trülnang of Jokhang and the Jowo Shakyamuni) are mentioned in inscriptions on that wall. I thank Amy Heller for drawing my attention to these inscriptions, which refer to both the Jowo Shakyamuni and the Nepalese queen.

21 Sönam Gyeltsen's *The Mirror Illuminating the Royal Genealogies*, ed. Sørensen, p. 194, n. 551.

22 Cf. Zhönnupel's *Blue Annals,* ed. G. Roerich and Gendün Chömpel, Varanasi/ Delhi, 1976, pp. 254, 488, 528, 603, 711, 801, and 1064. On p. 41, in connection with the shifting of the statue from Lhasa to Kyirong, Roerich understands the expression *"Lha-sa'i Jo-bo sKyi rong bskyal"* in the Tibetan text as referring to the more famous statue of the Buddha in the Jokhang of Lhasa.

23 For Pakpa's visit see Yang Shuwen et al., *Buddhist Thang-ka Art of Tibet: The Biographical Paintings of 'Phags pa*, Beijing/Lhasa, 1987, p. 152.

24 Cf. Kramer, pp. 31, 72–73 n. 124, and 85. Kramer follows Snellgrove in identifying this image with the Buddha.

25 Cf. for example D. Jackson, *The Mollas of Mustang: Historical, Religious and Oratorical Traditions of the Nepalese-Tibetan Borderland*, Dharamsala, 1984, p. 150, and F.-K. Ehrhard, "Tibetan Sources in Muktinath", *Ancient Nepal*, 134, July–August 1993, p. 30.

26 Slusser and Bishop, pp. 22–25, figs. 10–17.

27 A popular stupa cave object of pilgrimage in western Lo is described by Snellgrove, p. 189.

28 Together with Manidhara, the goddess Shadakshari is Shadakshara Lokeshvara's main assistant. The triad is described in the *Sadhanamala* and portrayed accordingly in the tantric pantheon (cf. M.-T. Mallmann, *Introduction à l'iconographie du tântrisme bouddhique*, Paris, 1975, p. 330, with Lokesh Chandra, *Buddhist Iconography*, New Delhi, 1991, p. 238, No. 612).

29 Cf. Slusser and Bishop, p. 23. The Newar artist Raja Kumar Shakya (b. 1966) from Lalitpur, in the Nepal Valley, made a large embossed and chased metal prayer-wheel for Möntang in the 1980s. More recently, Mukti Singh Thapa (b. 1957), a Nepalese painter now resident in Lalitpur, was involved in delicate restoration work at Möntang under Luigi Fieni's supervision.

30 Cf. chapter 1 on the temples of Möntang as well as chapter 7.

31 This hermitage and the river below it are referred to by the artificial name of "Sao" by P. Matthiessen, *East of Lo Monthang: In the Land of Mustang*, Boston, 1996, pp. 44, 47–51, 57, and 61 (the picture on p. 60 actually shows a cave north of Chödzong).

CHAPTER 4

Early Cave Paintings Rediscovered in Upper Lo

Luigi Fieni

For the first time in modern history, at the beginning of spring 2007, a team[1] of scholars, climbers, and explorers was able to gain access to several of the numerous human-excavated caves widely spread through the whole of Upper Lo. Using advanced mountaineering and abseiling techniques it was possible to enter caves otherwise out of reach. Among the several discoveries during the expedition was a cave with exquisite wall paintings never photographed before, nor viewed in modern times.

While camping in Möntang, the ancient capital of Lo, we asked the shepherds in the village as well as in the neighbouring settlements if they recalled areas containing caves with traces of colours on their walls. This inquiry led us to a nearby village called Tsoshar (or Choshar) where a shepherd had memories of a painted cave somewhere northeast of the village, a cave where he had found shelter during a rainstorm when he was younger.

After much scouting to find that spot we abseiled into what turned out to be the most important discovery of the expedition. Nobody had entered that cave for years, as proved by the fact that only snow leopard footprints were found on its floor. The shepherd realized that this was the cave he had sheltered in when he was just eight years old, from his signature scratched on the murals. At that time there had been a dangerous path leading to the cave. It was later completely eroded by wind, rain, and snow. He did not realize how important the discovery was, for the murals were for him just religious figures painted on a wall.

The cave is located at 4,114 metres above sea level. Soon after the discovery, the nearby villagers of Tsoshar named it Trakpuk Könchokling ("The Jewel Island Cave") after the nearby monastery. The cave lies ten metres down a cliff of one of the numerous clay "organ pipes",[2] not far from the remains of the monastery. Its location may also suggest its function as a retreat or meditation place for residents of the monastery.

The large entrance, which has partly collapsed as a result of erosion, leads to a rough rectangular chamber of about 54 square metres. Though this space is entirely empty, it hosts murals on its northern and western walls covering a surface of about 17 square metres. The painted area was once larger, but rain and snow have washed away a section of the right side; we can only guess what was once there.

A pentagonal niche in the northern side of the west wall, perhaps to host a missing statue or a teaching throne, divides the murals into three different iconographic cycles: the triad of Shadakshara Lokeshvara, Vajradhara, and Green Tara is found on the right of the niche; 17 portraits of lamas or religious masters on the northern wall; and two groups of mahasiddhas on either side.

A squared pillar, decorated with paintings belonging to the first cycle, is located nearly at the centre of the cave. The paintings are covered by a

4.1 Shadakshara Lokeshvara, Vajradhara, and Green Tara. Könchokling, 13th century. Distemper.

4.2 Lama presumably performing the consecration of the chapel. Könchokling, 13th century. Distemper.

thick leakage of clay, most probably caused by rain and melted snow coming in from above the collapsed entrance.

As for the first cycle, on the western wall to the right of the niche, the sequence of three deities with their attendants (figure 4.1) is painted in a manner that evokes the opulence of the Maitreya temple and of the hermitage of Chödzong discussed by Erberto Lo Bue in chapter 1. Although the paint is severely damaged, we can recognize Newar features which characterize some of the art of Lo. The proportions of the figures, slim and delicate, clearly recall a Newar influence. A richness of detail in the composition, the style of jewellery and flowers, as well as the wider palette including both blue and green, set the murals apart from the cycle of the mahasiddhas, although the style is not as elaborate as that found in the mature 14th–15th-century murals of Lo.

The second cycle on the northern wall and on an eastern indentation of the same is simply a sequence of lamas framed in various registers. While some of these are defaced, one depicts a lama performing a ceremony, possibly the consecration of the chapel (figure 4.2). The figures are drawn in a blank space with few details. Blue and green disappear from the palette and no inscriptions are present, thereby rendering attempts to identify these characters nearly impossible.

The third cycle is divided into two parts, one on the southern section of the western wall, the other on the eastern section of the northern wall, at the sides of the two cycles mentioned above. The majority of the extant figures is laid out on the western wall in a sequence of 63 panels, each approximately 35 to 45 centimetres wide, arranged in three rows of 21 panels (figure 4.3). The few images extant on the northern wall are laid out in two registers.

Below each portrait, an inscription in Tibetan script identifies the figure. In some cases, the character's origins are described along with his spiritual achievements. The entire sequence most probably belongs to the Sakya tradition, as the two great scholars Künga Nyingpo (1092–1158) and Sakya Pandita (1182–1251) are portrayed in it. Some faces have been selectively scratched away. Meticulous attention seems to have been given to the removal of some of the inscriptions.

Each composition is generally organized with a main figure assisted by an attendant in smaller proportions (to his right, on the western wall; and to his left, on the northern wall), with the smaller figures always portrayed in a gesture of offering (figures 4.4a and b). The siddhas are depicted in the rather free manner characterizing their iconography, in a space that is empty except for the presence of occasional trees and animals. Such emptiness within each

4.3 Partial view of the cycle of portraits of mahasiddhas. Könchokling, 13th century. Distemper.

frame is unusual in Indian, Newar, and Tibetan art. The gigantic images of the Mahamuni temple, the intricate mandalas of the Maitreya temple, the wrathful deities of the Chödzong cave, and the decorative elements of Luri and Trashi Geling with their cave temple stupas known locally as *kabum*,[3] all have in common a horror vacui, which is typical of the above-mentioned artistic traditions. This aversion to emptiness induced painters to create flowers, leaves, robe patterns, swirls, and roundels to fill empty spaces in a way that is reminiscent of the international Gothic style in medieval Europe. In contrast, the cycle of mahasiddhas in the cave of Könchokling does not show any of those features. The background of each panel is blank with no intricate motifs whatsoever.

4.4a Standing attendant. Könchokling, 13th century. Distemper.

4.4b The guru Ananta with a seated attendant. Könchokling, 13th century. Distemper.

In these blank spaces, trees and unusual animals are placed rather randomly. Though similar depictions of trees may be found in other murals in Lo, the portrayal of animals not found in this Himalayan region is remarkable. Ducks and monkeys are seen in the iconography of this cycle together with tigers, leopards, and other animals of the subtropics (figure 4.5). Their presence is intriguing because one would expect that the painter, given the relative freedom permitted in depicting scenes with mahasiddhas, would use motifs from his personal experience for the purpose of decoration. The depiction of these animals may indeed be a sign that the artist had come into contact with subtropical India or Nepal; indeed, he may have even come from those regions.

The use of red hues to shade the figures and give volume to the human bodies is another noteworthy characteristic of these paintings. When compared to the figures depicted in the ceiling of Luri stupa cave temple, the shading in the murals of Könchokling is much more primitive. Moreover, the human proportions are not as fine as those found in other 14th–15th-century painting in Lo. While the presence of Sakya Pandita implies that these murals cannot be earlier than the 13th century, the lack of richness in detail suggests a period previous to the 15th century.

As for the technique of execution, the murals were painted on top of two coatings of different plasters. The first preparatory layer, composed of pebbles, clay, and chopped straw, is only one centimetre thick and was meant to smooth the coarse surface of the cave. The second preparatory layer, composed of yellowish clay mixed with very tiny pebbles, is just a few millimetres thick and so much finer in granulometry[4] that it seems to have been sifted. To apply the plaster, the painters used an uneven tool, perhaps of stone or wood, for the surface of the wall appears to have been smoothed with irregular vertical strokes. The outer layer was whitewashed and subsequently the preparatory drawings were sketched. An odd sketch in the upper row depicts an ejaculating penis right behind a siddha's female attendant[5] (figure 4.6). The drawing was meant to be hidden by a layer of paint which has either vanished or become transparent through ageing. Although we were not allowed to take samples to analyse the nature of the pigments, we can state that the palette was poor, since important and expensive pigments such as malachite, azurite, and cinnabar are missing. Painters may have resorted to other pigments that have vanished with ageing. In general, the artists may have used clay-based ochres or oxides, which they could easily collect on site.

From a conservationist's point of view it is clear that the murals are in urgent need of restoration. The preparatory layers have separated randomly from the wall. To save these very important murals, careful re-adherence operations must be undertaken. In addition, because the paint layer now stands in direct sunlight much of the day, the pigments are suffering from gradual chemical alteration. Furthermore, the combination of wind erosion with rain and snow, and the impact of humans and animals over the centuries has caused loss of paint and scratches. To stop the ongoing deterioration, the murals should be protected from the elements, humans, and animals.

Other signs of deterioration document past activities within the cave. The presence of many holes in the upper section of the murals, for

4.5 Tiger next to a siddha. Könchokling, 13th century. Distemper.

instance, indicate the former presence of nails used possibly to hang objects like tangkas or curtains. Unfortunately new holes have been made recently by local devotees to hang prayer flags. The presence of soot from smoke may simply indicate the use of butter lamps in earlier times. Should experts in restoration programmes be engaged in the conservation of these remarkable murals, they would have to deal with issues of conservation as well as aesthetics.

The conservation of the Könchokling cave will depend on the way locals handle this important site. Just a few months after the discovery, nearby villagers were already leading groups of tourists into the cave. The tourists were permitted to take pictures and even touch the murals. Moreover, while abseiling was once required for entry, the cave is now accessible by a narrow path excavated into the mountain. In addition, a useless door has been set in one of the clay "organ pipes" leading to the cave. The problem is far from simple: should tourism be allowed to affect the conservation of such a historic site? Though this cave has survived for about seven centuries, its future existence is now at stake.

4.6 Female attendant with an original sketch showing an ejaculating penis. Könchokling, 13th century. Distemper.

FIGURE ACKNOWLEDGEMENTS
All photographs by Luigi Fieni.

NOTES
1   The team was partly funded by The North Face and Sky Door Productions, Bainbridge Island, WA, USA.
2   Common name used to define a specific erosion effect of mountain soil, as seen in figure 2.1.
3   Cf. M. Shepherd Slusser and L.M. Bishop, "Another Luri, A Newly Discovered Cave *Chorten* in Mustang", *Orientations*, 30/2, February 1999, p. 27: "According to local lore, the cave *chorten* at Trashi Geling qualifies as '*khabung*' *chorten*, a term unfamiliar to Tibetologists but defined in Mustang as a *chorten* erected by an individual in response to a divine command delivered in a dream or during meditation."
4   Measurement of grain sizes of sedimentary rocks.
5   The sketch is clearly executed under the paint layer and it is partly covered by the red colour of a pole, which did not vanish. It is located in the 12th panel of the upper row counting from left to right.

CHAPTER 5

Early Wall Paintings in Lo:
Luri Reconsidered

Helmut F. Neumann and Heidi A. Neumann

The hermitage of Luri lies in the valley of the Yara Khola, a side stream of the upper Kali Gandaki, which by cutting through the Himalayan chain has formed one of the deepest gorges in the world. Its greatest and earliest treasure, the Luri stupa, is situated high above the present monastery in a cave, cut into a pinnacle of the alluvial conglomerate rock which is characteristic of this considerably eroded landscape. The cave is accessible only by a steep path, which crosses the gorges along single tree-trunks.

In front of the main cave lies a small temple, which is used by a lama from the nearby village for religious ceremonies. A small opening in the wall of this temple room leads to a cave with an egg-shaped dome, replicating the form of the natural dome into which it was cut. Most of the space in the cave is taken up by a stupa (figure 5.1) leaving only a narrow path for circumambulation. Its highly polished surface gleams by the light of a small window in the east wall. The stupa is composed of the same elements as those in the Kathmandu Valley: a quadrangular base receding at the corners, a large hemispherical or dome-shaped central body surmounted by a cube and a succession of discs appearing as a spire, topped by an umbrella and a finial.

The surface of the Luri stupa has been used to present a painted iconographic programme. The red-painted base shows on each of its four sides, at the centre of the main facade, an image of one of the kings of the four cardinal directions. They are pictured standing with legs apart on a lotus base against the white background of a mandorla. On the north side, Vaishravana (figure 5.2) holds a jewel-spitting mongoose in his left hand and a jewelled sceptre in the right hand. He wears a bluish-green coat over a red robe, falling in large folds. His head, shoulders, and breast are protected by what resembles traditional Tibetan armour consisting of small iron plaques held together by strips of leather. The eight auspicious symbols are painted on the background of blue-green roundels on either side of the guardian kings (see figure 5.1).

The base recedes at the corners, creating eight approximately square spaces, on each of which is the depiction of a deity. Vaishravana is flanked by Penden Lhamo,[1] the first and the only female of the eight most important protectors of the dharma, on one side, and by a Jewel Goddess, one of the 12 guardian goddesses accompanying her, on the other. Penden Lhamo in blue rides on a pink mule through a sea of blood. The pensive mood on her face contrasts with the marks and symbols of her fierce nature: sword, trident, and the band of demon heads which hangs loosely over her shoulder. The saddle cover consists of a demon's skin, his head and arms hanging down.

The Jewel Goddess (figure 5.3), surrounded by flickering flames, rides a blue horse through an ocean of blood. She wears a red tunic with green

5.1 Luri stupa (east side). Circa late 13th century. Distemper.

lining, leaving her breasts uncovered. She holds a spear with both hands in addition to a staff. Her face, with wide open eyes, is encircled by a crown of skulls, and her black hair is bound into a chignon. The well-balanced composition strikes by its simplicity and carefully drawn details.

On the west side of the stupa base, a special form of Garuda (figure 5.4) sits on a nagini (female serpent deity), whose upper part resembles a human being, the lower part being that of a serpent. Garuda has a human body with the hooked beak and talons of a bird of prey. His special, often

5.2 Vaishravana. Base of stupa (north side), Luri. Circa late 13th century. Distemper.

5.3 Jewel Goddess. Base of stupa (north side), Luri. Circa late 13th century. Distemper.

hostile relationship to snakes is indicated by the naga around his shoulders and body, and by the small worshipping nagaraja protected by a snake hood. His body colours identify him as Jnana-Garuda: thigh down he is yellow (earth), his belly is white (water), his upper body red (fire), his head blue (air), and his wings are many-coloured (space).

The dome of the stupa carries images of the goddess Ushnishavijaya, and of the bodhisattvas Vajrapani and Shadakshara Lokeshvara. Ushnishavijaya (figures 5.1 and 5.5), as the primary image, faces the entrance of the cave and is distinguished by a larger size and the accompanying retinue of her mandala: two bodhisattvas and four protective deities. She is the bearer of three sadhanas, magic practices assuring fulfilment of wishes, and is specifically worshipped to prolong life. Her representation on a stupa has been a fundamental element of the Bhimaratha ceremony, in which gratitude is expressed to her when a man reaches the canonical age of 77 years, seven months, and seven days; such long life allows him the accumulation of a great number of merits to ensure a better incarnation.[2]

Ushnishavijaya is depicted in Luri in her most familiar manifestation: three-faced, with central white and left yellow faces serene, and the right blue face fierce; in the prime of her youth; clad in divine garments; adorned with exquisite jewellery. Her gestures and attributes are those almost invariably connected to her iconography. She is accompanied by the white bodhisattva Avalokiteshvara (figure 5.6) on her right and the blue bodhisattva Vajrapani on her left. As the head of the lotus family, Avalokiteshvara holds the stem of a lotus flower in his left hand. Vajrapani, as the head of the vajra (thunderbolt weapon) family, is usually depicted holding a vajra. In this particular representation, however, he holds a lotus flower supporting a small vajra.

Below Ushnishavijaya's lotus throne, there are four protective deities encircled by a garland. They are the four krodhas, wrathful aspects of the dharmapala (guardian of dharma) protecting the Ushnishavijaya mandala. Their bodies are painted in different shades of blue, and their only garment is a tigerskin around the hips. They menacingly brandish weapons in their raised right hands, and hold slings in their left hands.

On the opposite side of the dome dwells Shadakshara Lokeshvara, the patron of Tibet and as such one of its most popular deities, incarnated in the great Tibetan king Songtsen Gampo as well as in the Dalai Lamas. Invariably four-armed, his main hands are joined in front of the breast in the gesture of adoration and salutation. The secondary right hand holds the rosary, the secondary left the lotus, in which a small diamond is embedded.

On the north side of the stupa a fierce form of Vajrapani (figure 5.7) was painted on the dome in a particularly well-balanced composition. In his special form of Chanda-maharoshana Vajrapani,[3] he is dark blue, has three eyes, hair blazing like fire, bared fangs, and holds a vajra in his raised right hand and a ghanta (bell) in his left hand by his side. He stands with his left leg extended in a forceful (alidha) posture, seemingly indifferent to the nagas that crawl in his hair, one winding itself around the earring.

5.4 Jnana-Garuda. Base of stupa (west side), Luri. Circa late 13th century. Distemper.

Above the dome, the cubical harmika carries small paintings of the four transcendental Buddhas on the appropriate sides: Amitabha (west), Ratnasambhava (south), Akshobhya (east), and Amoghasiddhi (north). A lotus supports the umbrella at the top of the stupa, its petals containing pictures of the eight Medicine Buddhas (figure 5.8). Despite their small size, each Medicine Buddha is clearly rendered, allowing identification on the basis of body colours and mudras (gestures). For example, the supreme physician, Bhaisajyaguru, blue in colour (figure 5.8, right), holds a twig of the myrobalan, whose dried fruit is used in traditional medicine.

5.5 Ushnishavijaya. Dome of stupa (east side), Luri. Circa late 13th century. Distemper.

5.6 Avalokiteshvara accompanying Ushnishavijaya. Dome of stupa (east side), Luri. Circa late 13th century. Distemper.

5.7 Chanda-maharoshana Vajrapani. Dome of stupa (north side), Luri. Circa late 13th century. Distemper.

On the ceiling of the cave, surrounding the lotus and flame circles of the mandala, is a group of eight mahasiddhas, each encircled by a roundel formed by a creeping vine. Mahasiddhas are usually represented in Tibet as a group of 84. The mahasiddhas in Luri form a particular subgroup of eight, the earliest examples of which are attributable to the early 13th century and most frequently, if not exclusively, to a Kagyüpa context.[4] This group comprises siddhas whose teachings were of particular importance to Tibet, but exemplifies also their variety of types: the yogin, the monk, the king. The representation of the eight siddhas at Luri follows a counter-clockwise sequence. Indrabhuti (figure 5.9), the enlightened king, is represented sitting on a simple throne platform supported by lion's paws, hinting at his royal status. He wears a red dhoti and a scarf is bound around his hair, falling

5.8 Medicine Buddhas. Paintings under the stupa umbrella, Luri. Circa late 13th century. Distemper.

over his shoulders. His smiling face is framed by earrings with vajra design and a simple bejewelled necklace. A meditation cord goes around his waist and knee, a reminder of the fact that he became a yogin after abdicating the throne.

Dombi Heruka (figure 5.10), riding on a tigress, is also of royal descent. The snake in his hair reminds us that he used a poisonous snake as a whip when he returned from the forest with his wife and tantric consort, the daughter of a dombi, a low-class musician. While this explains the first part of his name, the second part alludes to his transformation into a manifestation of Hevajra at the end of his life.

Some mahasiddhas were originally Buddhist monks, but only Nagarjuna (figure 5.11) is always pictured in a monk's robe. Meditating with his hands making the teaching gesture, he is protected by four snakes winding around to make a seat for him, their heads forming a hood over his head. The monk's staff and bowl on either side complete this harmonious composition.

Mahasiddha Ghantapa (figure 5.12) wears a small crown, a reminder of his royal descent. Holding a vajra and a ghanta in his raised hands, he is shown at the very time of taking off to fly through the air, a decisive moment in his biography, just before he appeared as Chakrasamvara with his consort as Vajravarahi. His fascinating life story combines his keeping vows as a monk at Nalanda with years of meditation as a yogin renouncing worldly pleasures, but with a decisive erotic episode in which he gains his tantric consort.

Kukkuripa (figure 5.13) is always pictured with his dog, even in series in which the other seven mahasiddhas are shown with their female consorts. This is related to the episode in his life when he returned to earth from the heaven of the 33 gods, since he could not forget his dog whom he had left behind. When he petted her, she turned into a dakini (tantric deity) who subsequently taught him the union of wisdom (female) with method (male), thereby enabling Kukkuripa to obtain the highest siddhi ("perfection").

Opposite
5.9 Mahasiddha Indrabhuti. Cave ceiling, Luri. Circa late 13th century. Distemper.
5.10 Mahasiddha Dombi Heruka. Cave ceiling, Luri. Circa late 13th century. Distemper.
5.11 Mahasiddha Nagarjuna. Cave ceiling, Luri. Circa late 13th century. Distemper.
5.12 Mahasiddha Ghantapa. Cave ceiling, Luri. Circa late 13th century. Distemper.

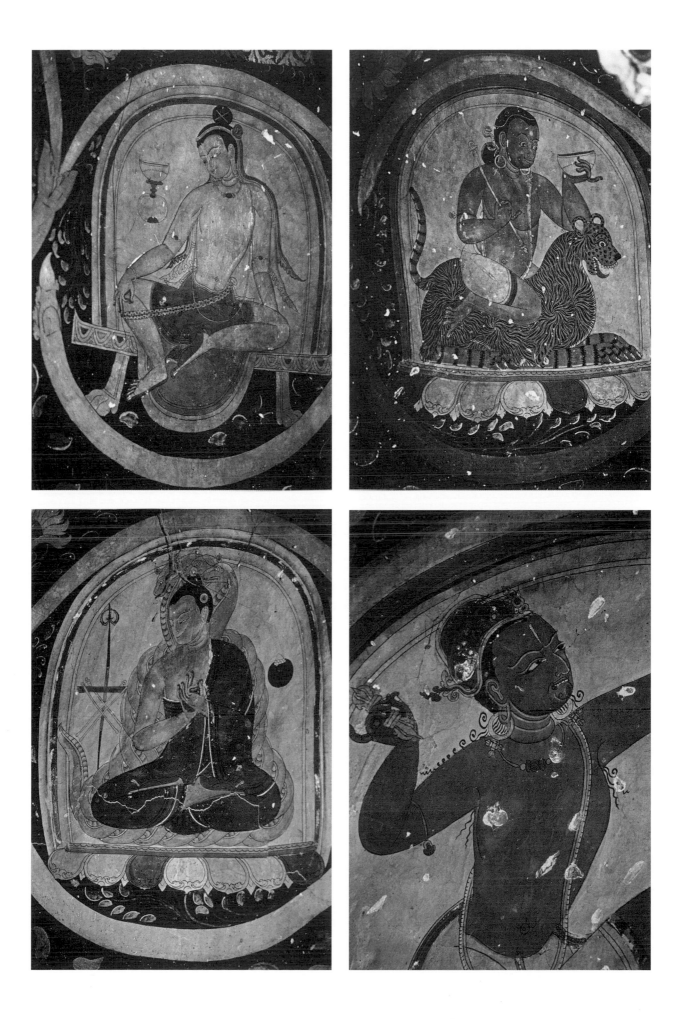

5.13 Mahasiddha Kukkuripa. Cave ceiling, Luri. Circa late 13th century. Distemper.

5.14 Mahasiddha Padmavajra. Cave ceiling, Luri. Circa late 13th century. Distemper.

Seated on a lotus rising out of the water, Mahasiddha Padmavajra (figure 5.14) is portrayed wearing a yellow cap, a red dhoti, and a red shawl whose ends are wound around his arms and float freely to his sides, well balancing the simple composition.

The painting of Luyipa[5] is perhaps the most accomplished in the group, his pensive mood well captured in his delicately drawn face. Luyipa is almost invariably shown eating the intestines of raw fish which fishermen discard on the banks of the Ganga. He thus liberated himself from the notion of distinguishing between good and bad, his last impediment to obtaining siddhi.

In the last portrait the hunter Shavaripa (figure 5.15) sits cross-legged on a lotus. On his back he carries two quivers, held by strings of pearls, which are joined at the centre of his breast by a white medallion. This iconography combines Shavaripa's past as a hunter with his transformation into a practising yogin, abstaining from meat thanks to lessons which he received miraculously from Avalokiteshvara.

The images of the mahasiddhas excel in the originality of their composition and the use of fine line combined with restrained shading. They are the result of a great artistic sensitivity, exceptional in Tibetan art of their period. There are no stylistic precedents for this group, masterpieces of early Tibetan painting, and also among the earliest representations of the eight siddhas in Tibetan art.

From the 14th century on, particularly for the purpose of inclusion in the eight charnel grounds[6] which surround mandalas, especially those of the Anuttarayoga class, Padmavajra was replaced by Virupa. This occurred concomitantly with the rise of the Sakyapa's power in Tibet, Virupa's teachings constituting the core philosophy of this school. While today traditional Sakya colours are conspicuous on houses and temples in Lo, the wall paintings of Luri make a Kagyüpa affiliation of that site appear more probable. On the west wall of the cave, above the larger paintings of a monk, Buddha Shakyamuni, Vajradhara, and Vajrasattva, is a row of seated monks. According to a recent report,[7] this row starts with the figure of Marpa. But at least since 1992, when the authors of this article visited Luri, there was a clear indication of a fifth painting to the left of the monk, and although damaged beyond recognition, there must have been at least two figures in the lineage before Marpa. The logical guess would be Tilopa and Naropa, the two mahasiddhas preceding Marpa in the Kagyüpa lineage.

The primordial Buddha Vajradhara (figure 5.16), who precedes Tilopa in the Kagyü lineage, is painted as a large seated figure below the lineage of monks that follow Marpa. Vajradhara is light blue in colour, wears the threefold bejewelled crown, and sits in the meditative posture, holding vajra and ghanta, with arms crossed in front of his chest. His face is rendered with exquisite sensitivity and refinement.

He is followed by the white Vajrasattva (figure 5.17), holding the same attributes, but differently: the vajra held vertically in the right hand in front of his chest, and the ghanta upside down in the left hand above the corresponding thigh. The end of this row is taken by the blue protective deity Achala, brandishing a sword above his head. At the other end Vajradhara is preceded by a monk wearing a red cap (figure 5.18) and by Shakyamuni with his two best disciples. The prominent position of the monk suggests that he might be the founder of Luri hermitage. His facial features are individualistic and he holds his hands in the gesture of religious instruction. He wears a garment showing a prominent armhole and is protected by an outer sitting robe characteristic of Tibetan monks' portraits of the 13th–14th century.[8]

Stylistically, the paintings of the mahasiddhas at Luri are unique. The other paintings on the walls of the cave and those on the stupa share many features, both with Newar religious paintings on cloth (paubhas) of the 13th century and with Tibetan wall paintings of the early 14th century, particularly in Zhalu monastery. A close similarity exists to the earliest known paubhas, one depicting Ratnasambhava and acolytes in the Los Angeles County Museum of Art, which has been dated by Pratapaditya Pal to the early 13th century on stylistic grounds,[9] and its pair, depicting Amitabha Buddha with acolytes in the Museum of Fine Arts in Boston.[10] The features of face and body and particularly the crown and body jewellery of the Vajradhara in figure 5.16 resemble those of the Buddhas in the two paubhas, even in the details of the shape of the ornaments and the placement of the jewels therein. The similarity extends to the garments worn by the bodhisattvas attending on Ushnishavijaya in even such small details as their slightly mannered undulating hemline (see figure 5.6). A similar white

5.15 Mahasiddha Shavaripa. Cave ceiling, Luri. Circa late 13th century. Distemper.

undulating line is found on the cloth which borders the carpet hanging off the throne-back of Vajrasattva (see figure 5.17), and is also found in the paubhas mentioned above.

At the same time, looking at the features which the Luri murals share with the wall paintings at Zhalu monastery, notably those of the corridor surrounding the temple of Prajnaparamita, it becomes clear that those of Luri are slightly less evolved and therefore probably earlier, particularly since they have comparable artistic merit. From these observations a late 13th-century date may be suggested for the Luri wall paintings.

Following the publications on the iconography[11] and style[12] of the paintings at Luri hermitage, Mary Slusser discovered the stupa cave temple of Trashi Geling, just a few kilometres below Luri, in the same valley.[13] In iconography, style, and period, Trashi Geling shows kinship with Luri. The stupa has or retains only the regents of the four directions and the eight auspicious symbols. Shadakshara Lokeshvara and an enthroned monk[14] are the only major paintings on the walls. Though they share many stylistic elements with the figures at Luri, they reveal a more elaborate rendering of the decorative elements. The Trashi Geling murals show a few stylistic elements which are absent in Luri, but well-known from 13th/14th-century Tibetan painting, such as the tails of the animals on the throne-back ending as scrollwork around the halo of the main figure. Moreover, both the colour scheme and the line of the drawing in the Trashi Geling paintings are less accomplished.

Quite different is the case of the wall paintings discovered more recently in the cave hermitage of Könchokling, in Upper Lo, and documented by Luigi Fieni in chapter 4. There the hairstyle, crown, and jewellery of bare-breasted lady attendants compare well with the Avalokiteshvara attending on Ushnishavijaya in Luri, their breasts resembling those of the Luri Jewel Goddess. Yet, some of their faces, despite similarities in the details of features, give the impression of an earlier period, perhaps the second half of the 13th century, and so does the striped dhoti of the lady attendant. In view of the absence of records for the early history of Lo, nothing is known about the foundation of Luri. As has been explained above, a Kagyüpa affiliation appears probable because of the presence of portraits of masters of that tradition on the west wall of the cave. A more recent and specific Karma Kagyü connection can be made out from the clay portraits of three Black Hat lamas in the small temple room in front of the cave.

Perhaps the iconographic programme painted on the walls of the cave will in the future allow the affiliation of Luri to be defined more precisely, as well as the reason and purpose for which it was established. The following serendipitous finding may be a first step in that direction: the main deities, painted on the dome of the stupa in Luri, are Ushnishavijaya, Shadakshara Lokeshvara, and Chanda-maharoshana Vajrapani. The same triad occupies an important position in a roughly contemporary cave in the Sutlej Valley some 400 kilometres northwest of Luri. The central wall of that cave shows a row of nine deities below the group of the eight Medicine Buddhas and

5.16 Vajradhara. West wall of cave, Luri.
Circa late 13th century. Distemper.
5.17 Vajrasattva. West wall of cave, Luri.
Circa late 13th century. Distemper.

5.18 Portrait of a monk. West wall of cave,
Luri. Circa late 13th century. Distemper.

Prajnaparamita: the five Jinas and the three deities mentioned above (i.e. Ushnishavijaya surrounded by the deities of her mandala, Shadakshara Lokeshvara, and Chanda-maharoshana Vajrapani), besides Namasangiti Manjushri, a light red form of Manjushri with four arms.

The prominent position of those three deities (including the same manifestations of Avalokiteshvara and Vajrapani) both in Luri and in this other cave cannot be a mere coincidence. It might be speculated that the painting on the south side of the Luri stupa, which was lost when the cave wall crumbled, represented Namasangiti Manjushri. This group of deities must have played a very important role in the religious life of the masters who conceived the iconographic programme in these caves. While at the present time we can only admire the beauty of these wall paintings high up in the cliffs of steep mountains, their deeper religious meaning still remains a mystery.

FIGURE ACKNOWLEDGEMENTS
All photographs courtesy Helmut and Heidi Neumann.

NOTES
1   I. Alsop, "The Wall Paintings of Lo", *Nepal: Old Images, New Insights*, ed. P. Pal, Mumbai, 2004, pp. 128–39, fig. 2.
2   P. Pal, "The Bhimaratha Rite and Nepali Art", *Oriental Art*, 23/2, Summer 1977, pp. 176–89.
3   L. Chandra, *Dictionary of Buddhist Iconography*, Vol. 14, Delhi, 2005, p. 4025.
4   C. Luczanits, "The Eight Great Siddhas in Early Tibetan Painting", *Holy Madness*, ed. R. Linrothe, New York, 2006, p. 78.
5   Alsop, p. 129, fig. 1.
6   H.F. Neumann, "Cremation Grounds in Early Tibetan Mandalas", *Orientations*, 33/10, 2002, pp. 42–50.
7   Alsop, p. 130.
8   M.M. Rhie and R.A.F. Thurman, *Wisdom and Compassion, the Sacred Art of Tibet*, London, 1991, p. 255. E. Lo Bue, in *Images of Faith: A Private Collection of Himalayan Art,* ed. A.M. and F. Rossi, London, 2008, p. 15, fig. 13.
9   P. Pal, *Art of Nepal*, Los Angeles, 1985, p. 60, P7; see also Steven Kossak, *Painted Images of Enlightenment: Early Tibetan Thankas, 1050–1450*, Mumbai, 2010, p. 160, fig. 107.
10   P. Pal, *The Arts of Nepal*, Leiden, 1978, pl. 70; see also Kossak, pp. 95–96, fig. 63.
11   H.F. Neumann, "The Wall Paintings of the Luri Gonpa", *Orientations*, 25/2, 1994, pp. 79–91.
12   H.F. Neumann, "Paintings of the Luri Stupa in Lo", *Tibetan Art*, ed. J. Casey Singer and P. Denwood, London, 1997, pp. 178–85.
13   M. Shepherd Slusser and L.M. Bishop, "Another Luri: A Newly Discovered Cave Chorten in Lo, Nepal", *Orientations*, 30/2, 1999, pp. 18–27.
14   Ibid., pp. 25–26.

CHAPTER 6

Wonders of Möntang

Erberto Lo Bue

During the 15th century, under Amapel and his successors, Lo went through a period of economic and cultural growth whose importance is inversely proportional to its duration. Like other princes in Tibet – and their contemporaries in central and northern Italy – the rulers of Lo were eager to celebrate their newly acquired power by sponsoring the making of religious buildings and images, in order to accumulate merit and also to make up for the sins they committed in eliminating their enemies, as had been the case since the time of Ashoka in India and even under Buddhist rulers in early Tibet. Thus the establishment of Amapel's dynasty was glorified through the construction of the temples of Maitreya and Mahamuni at Möntang, which entailed the production of murals vying with the finest wall paintings in the more famous monastery and Great Stupa at Gyantsé, in southwest Tibet.

In Lo, as had been the case in geo-cultural Tibet and elsewhere, the building and decoration of temples and monasteries also represented a conscious effort by rulers to strengthen religion, providing an ethical as well as social frame for their rule through the establishment of privileged relationships with, and thanks to the support of, particularly authoritative religious figures. Like the rulers of Western Tibet in the 11th, of Zhalu in the 13th, and of Gyantsé in the 15th century, Amapel and his son invited prominent religious masters to institutionalize Buddhism on doctrinal grounds both through the erection of temples and monasteries, and through the representation of specific iconographic programmes in the region they had come to rule. Like the kings of Gyantsé and the princes of Zhalu, the rulers of Lo chiefly followed the Sakya tradition, and became admirers of Künga Zangpo, the famous scholar and founder of Ngor monastery (Ngor Evam Chönden) mentioned in chapter 1, though they also supported the Nyingma and Kagyü orders. The preference accorded to Künga Zangpo had far-reaching consequences for the art of Lo.

An admirer of Newar art, Künga Zangpo invited Newar painters to decorate the temples in the monastery he founded at Ngor in 1429, two years after his first visit to Lo. During their journey from the Nepal Valley to Ngor, Newar artists stopped and worked at various sites, including Shekar and Sakya, but their eagerness to oblige Künga Zangpo made them disregard an offer of gold to work at an important Bön centre in southwest Tibet. At the monastery of Ngor Newar artists painted 11 great compositions portraying the masters of Künga Zangpo's religious lineage, and also fashioned several gilded statues of Shakyamuni and of the Buddhas of the Ten Directions.[1] We know the names of two in a team of six Newar artists that worked at Ngor: Vanguli and Akheraja.[2] Künga Zangpo's extensive recourse to Newar painters contributes to explain a Tibetan scholarly tradition according to which the painting style of the Nepal Valley dominated in Tibet until the first half of the 15th century.

6.1 Tantric goddess. Maitreya temple, Möntang, 1440s. Distemper.

Künga Zangpo's preference for Newar artists may explain why in the temples and chapels of Lo one comes across murals, metal sculptures, and even book covers fashioned in Newar style from the 15th century onwards.[3] Giuseppe Tucci reported that the monastery of Tsarang used to be a true "art gallery" with Newar, Tibetan, as well as Indian statues and painted scrolls. At the time of his visit in 1952, dozens of such valuable scrolls were thrown higgledy-piggledy into a basket and soiled by the droppings of hens that used to brood over them. Tucci explained that Tsarang monastery's "lazy" abbot, a son of the raja of Mustang, was assisted by two or three "very ignorant" monks.[4]

In the fire female dragon year corresponding to 1437, by order of Agön Zangpo, master carpenters and masons started the construction of the temple that only in the 17th century came to be called "Jampa Tsuklakhang" ("Main Temple of Maitreya"). The construction was completed in the fire female hare year corresponding to 1447. Its murals were painted by expert masters from Lo, Dölpo, the Nepal Valley, and Gungtang,[5] the area mentioned in chapter 1, forming part of the Kali Gandaki headwaters and bordering with Lo, and now included in Kyirong county, southwest Tibet. Three inscriptions under as many goddesses painted in the circumambulation corridor of the temple refer to the great master – not a female painter as believed by some[6] – Gyeltsen from Gungtang, who painted the Sitatapatra illustrated in Luigi Fieni's contribution on the restoration of the temple of Maitreya (figure 8.2), and perhaps also the goddess painted on the same wall and illustrated here (figure 6.1).

The temple and its main image were consecrated in 1448, but the original sculpture was not the painted clay statue to be seen today, which was consecrated in 1663 and restored in recent years[7] (see figure 8.11). The reason for such replacement is not clear, but it should be pointed out that Lo, like the rest of the Himalayan region and the Indian subcontinent in general, has suffered from earthquakes such as the devastating one of 1505, which destroyed not only monastic buildings, temples, and statues, but even forests and fruit trees.[8]

Huge statues of Maitreya have been produced for a long time in areas belonging to the Tibetan cultural sphere, notably in Ladakh.[9] In Tibet proper the Kashmiri Pandita Shakyashribhadra sponsored the erection of a large image of Maitreya at the monastery of Tropuk and consecrated it in 1212, before travelling to Gungtang and Lo during his return journey to Kashmir.[10] Large statues of Maitreya are found elsewhere in Lo, for example in a private chapel at Kagbeni as well as in the monastery of Tsarang.[11]

In terms of aesthetic quality and style, the Yoga tantra mandalas painted on the walls of the first floor in the temple of Maitreya in the 1440s match those painted in the Temple of the "Divine Palace" (Vimana) crowning the main monastic building of Gyantsé about a score of years earlier, in 1425,[12] one year after the dharmaraja of Gyantsé had been entrusted by the Sakya rulers with the protection of their main seat. The Anuttarayoga tantra mandalas painted on the walls of the Vimana chapel crowning the temple of Maitreya are, in spite of their complexity, of an inferior quality and, like some wall paintings on the ground floor, were executed at the close of the 15th century.[13]

Iconographic programmes featuring mandalas have been a characteristic of the Sakya tradition, including the school of the monastery of Ngor, for which Künga Zangpo asked Newar artists to paint a complete set of mandalas of the Vajravali cycle along with three additional mandalas from the 12th-century *Kriyasamucchaya* collection during the period 1429–56.[14] It should be mentioned that the great scholar of Ngor was an advocate of the practice of the Kriya and Charya tantras at a time when such texts were no longer so popular in Tibet, and that his extensive research in tantric sources represented the basis of a much later compilation, the "Compendium of Tantras", a famous text describing 139 mandalas which were accordingly painted in Eastern Tibet during the second half of the 19th century.[15] The iconographic plan of the temple of Maitreya is described in a brief passage found by David Jackson in an unpublished genealogy of Lo, specifying that the ground floor is related to sutra teachings and lower tantras, the middle one to Yoga tantras, and the upper one to Anuttarayoga tantra teachings. Thus, as in the Great Stupa of Gyantsé and in the three-storey cave temple No. 12 at Ellora well before that, the structure of the temple of Maitreya embodies and symbolizes a doctrinal progression.[16]

The painters who worked at Möntang followed the iconography and iconometry afforded by the Tibetan translations of Buddhist texts from India – which by then were available in the monastic libraries of Lo – or by their commentaries, painting their compositions presumably under the direction of expert supervisors, as had been the case at Gyantsé. Their artistic idiom betrays the Newar rendition of Indian aesthetics, which were particularly appreciated in the Sakya environment, where even Dandin's famous treatise

6.2 Detail of Vajradhatu mandala, by Devananda. Maitreya temple, Möntang, 1440s. Distemper.

6.3 Bodhisattva. Mahamuni temple,
Möntang, 1440s. Distemper.

on poetic composition, the *Kavyadarsha* ("Mirror of Poetry"), had been
translated, becoming very popular in Tibetan scholarly circles along with the
translations of famous Indian classics.[17] Indeed, the Vajradhatu mandala, the
finest of all in the temple of Maitreya, at the southern end of the west wall
on the first floor (figure 6.2), was painted by the Newar master Devananda,
as reported by the inscription below the composition, and that painter is
likely to have been the most authoritative in the team of artists attending to
the decoration of the whole floor, if not their leader.

The usage of placing figures in niches consisting of multilobate arches
supported by columns made up of superimposed stems (see figures 8.2 and
8.3), of inserting secondary images in medallions (see figures 8.2, 8.7, and

8.8, and figures 9.1–9.3 and 9.11), and of resorting to deep shades of colour, link the style of the murals in the temple of Maitreya with the Newar idiom adopted pervasively at Gyantsé and, before that, at the monasteries of Sakya, Ngor, and even Zhalu, an important principality that had not only entertained close family ties with the rulers of Sakya and Gyantsé, but also benefited from the patronage of a king of the Nepal Valley in the 11th and of the Yuan emperors of China in the 14th century.

As at Gyantsé, the spaces between the larger mandalas are occupied by smaller mandalas, whereas the remaining spaces house images of Buddhas, bodhisattvas, and religious masters (see figures 8.5, 8.6, 8.8, and 8.10). Some of the latter (for instance the pair of lamas seated at the sides of Parnashavari's head in figure 8.4) are shown wearing the same sort of baggy cloak with wide pleats – the depiction of pleating being ultimately of Gandharan origin – found also in some portraits in the cave hermitage of Könchokling (cf. figure 4.2), a feature that is usually associated with Kagyü portraiture, but is found here in a Sakya context and lasts in Tibetan painting until at least the 15th century.

The other main temple in Möntang is dedicated to Tupchen, namely Shakyamuni under his epithet of "Great Sage" (Mahamuni). Its foundations were laid by King Tsangchen Trashigön in 1468 and the temple was

6.4 Attendant Bodhisattva. Mahamuni temple, Möntang, 1440s. Distemper.

6.5 Attendant Bodhisattva. Mahamuni temple, Möntang, 1440s. Distemper.

6.6 Textile pattern. Mahamuni temple, Möntang, 1440s. Distemper.

6.7 Textile pattern. Mahamuni temple, Möntang, 1440s. Distemper.

completed in 1472.[18] It was consecrated by the Great Pandita Shakya Chokden (1428–1507), a famous scholar especially invited for that occasion, with the performance of important ceremonies during a large religious gathering.[19]

Vairochana, as identified by an inscription on the wall, is painted above the entrance door, facing east, while teaching the doctrine (see figure 9.1), hence making the same gesture displayed by Mahamuni, who is found at the opposite side of the assembly hall and to whom the temple is dedicated. In Buddhist iconography Vairochana occupies the central position in the pentad of the cosmic Buddhas and his presence at the centre of this wall might also have a political meaning, signifying the traditional association between Tibetan rulers and this Buddha, as in the case of the

6.8 Flower decorations. Mahamuni temple, Möntang, 1440s. Distemper.

important image of Vairochana housed in the chapel, also facing east, on the fifth storey of the Great Stupa of Gyantsé.[20] The cosmic Buddha is flanked by two bodhisattvas and furthermore assisted by the Eight Great Bodhisattvas – three painted on either side of the same wall and two on the northern and southern walls respectively – each of them being in turn flanked by a pair of attendants (see figure 9.2). The other images painted on the southern wall include the five cosmic Buddhas as well as Amitayus and Mahamuni, who is depicted again at the southern end of the western wall in a larger composition with gorgeous details.

Bodhisattvas and attendants are painted with care (figures 6.3 6.5), and so are the motifs of various garments, reflecting a familiarity with luxurious textiles (figures 6.6 and 6.7; cf. figure 9.9) imported from various parts of Asia, as well as the decoration of the thrones and background (figure 6.8), comparing well with the quality of the best murals found at Gyantsé. Minor figures are drawn in a lively manner (figure 6.12; cf. figure 9.8) and the colour scheme of the plumage of some mythical animals, Garudas, and kirtimukhas (lit. "face of glory") (figures 6.9–6.11 and 6.13; cf. figure 9.7) is reminiscent of that of the streaked feathers of Garudas painted in the murals of some temples in the main monastery at Zhalu.[21]

The statue of Mahamuni, to whom the temple is dedicated, is placed at centre in the western section of the assembly hall, flanked by those of Shadakshara Lokeshvara and Manjushri. That triad is in turn flanked by images of Vajradhara and Padmasambhava, the famous tantric guru from the Swat Valley. In Tucci's time the statue of Vajradhara was apparently replaced by an image of Vaishravana, the regent of the north and the god of wealth, perhaps hinting at the economic status and strategic position of Lo at the time of the construction of this temple, performing the same role as the representation of Vaishravana in the ancient vestibule of the Golden Temple at Zhalu.[22]

The painters who attended to the decoration of this temple – presumably from 1469 to 1472 – enjoyed a high reputation, being qualified

6.9 Mythical bird. Mahamuni temple, Möntang, 1440s. Distemper.

6.10 Mythical animal. Mahamuni temple, Möntang, 1440s. Distemper.

Opposite
6.11 Garuda. Mahamuni temple, Möntang, 1440s. Distemper.

in the inscriptions as "skilled with their hands" and "skilled in the art of painting".[23] In the highly ornate language of such inscriptions, based on the Indian tradition of the "alamkara" (symbolic imagery), several expressions hint at the members of the royal family and of the latter's entourage by means of allusions and puns, as is often the case in this kind of literature, which in 15th-century Tibet was exemplified by the ornate verses found in the inscriptions on the walls of the temples at Gyantsé and also in the text recording the history of the dynasty that had them built.[24] Another figure mentioned by the inscriptions in the temple of Mahamuni in connection with its erection is Chönyi Zangpo, perhaps an epithet hinting at Chönyi Senggé, the great abbot of the kingdom of Western Tibet in the [15th?] century.[25] Like the wall

6.12 Lion with a human figure. Mahamuni temple, Möntang, 1440s. Distemper.

6.13 Garuda. Mahamuni temple, Möntang, 1440s. Distemper.

paintings in the temple of Maitreya, those in the temple of Mahamuni reflect the style of the murals painted at Gyantsé from 1420 to 1439 by artists still influenced by Newar, hence ultimately Indian, aesthetics, with the figures of bodhisattvas "posing", rather than "acting", in conformity with the theories on drama as expressed in Bharata's *Natyashastra*, whereby the onlooker ought to savour the "rasa" of emotions, rather than the emotions themselves.

Artistic activity in Lo continued during the following century and murals in a temple at Tsarang were commissioned in 1545 by a lama from neighbouring Dölpo, which at the time paid taxes to Lo,[26] but by the 17th century the great artistic season that had flourished in Lo two centuries before was waning. In 1952 Tucci predicted that – like many of the temples he had surveyed in Ladakh and Tibet in the 1930s and 1940s – those of Maitreya and Mahamuni at Möntang, too, would eventually disappear after his visit.[27]

Fortunately, Tucci's prediction has proved wrong in this case; however, several ancient sites in Lo are actually in ruins,[28] in spite of the fact that the region was not plagued by the Cultural Revolution. In the past 500 years no local artists have been able to compete with the masters that decorated its foremost temples, reflecting the cultural decadence that has characterized geo-cultural Tibet in the last centuries. Still, thanks to the restoration work undertaken since the end of the 1990s by the American Himalayan Foundation, which has sponsored an important project of conservation in the temples of Maitreya and Mahamuni, presently under Luigi Fieni's direction, we are today in a position to admire the wonders of Lo. For several years a team of local young people, including women, has been trained to restore and maintain the paintings in those two temples. In spite of the indifference, sometimes hostility, of the authorities in Kathmandu, the restorers sponsored by the American Himalayan Foundation have succeeded in involving the local community in this project, making it aware of the importance of its artistic heritage. They have, furthermore, renewed Lo's ancient artistic bond with Nepal by inviting an outstanding Nepalese painter, Mukti Singh Thapa, to work in the temples where at least one of his predecessors, Devananda, had distinguished himself so singularly over five centuries earlier.

FIGURE ACKNOWLEDGEMENTS
All photographs by Luigi Fieni.

NOTES

1   L. Petech in A. Ferrari, *Mk'yen brtse's Guide to the Holy Places of Central Tibet*, Roma, 1958, p. 147, n. 475.

2   Cf. G. Tucci, *Tibetan Painted Scrolls*, Kyoto, 1980, p. 277; and *Tibet: Land of Snows*, London, 1967, p. 100; with D. Jackson, *A History of Tibetan Painting: The Great Tibetan Painters and Their Traditions*, Wien, 1996, pp. 82 and 87, n. 183.

3   Cf. P. Matthiessen, *East of Lo Monthang: In the Land of Mustang*, Boston, 1996, pp. 136–37, where the inscription on a fine parcel-gilt silver book cover reports the names of two craftsmen, Rup Tej and Abhaya Jyoti, father and son, who have been discussed by Amy Heller in chapter 7.

4   G. Tucci, *Tra giungle e pagode*, Roma, 1979, p. 109. The book was translated into English and published under the misleading title of *Journey to Mustang*.

5   Cf. R.K. Dhungel, *The Kingdom of Lo (Mustang): A Historical Study*, Kathmandu, 2002, pp. 239–40 and 244; and *Bkra shis bstan 'dzin, Glo ljongs chos kyi zhing sar bstan pa 'phel rim gyi dkar chag dwangs shel me long*, Kathmandu, 2001, pp. 99–100. The dates provided by the latter source are consistently wrong by a cycle of 60 years, as it appears from the notes in the appendix, where the 7th cycle replaces the 6th in the text.

6   In an art-historical context the Tibetan compound word *dpon mo che* does not mean "great lady", but "great master painter" and as such it appears regularly in front of painters' names in texts as well as inscriptions, for example under the murals in the Great Stupa of Gyantsé.

7   See R. Vitali, "On Byams pa and Thub chen lha khang of Glo sMos thang", *The Tibet Journal*, XXIV/1, 1999, pp. 18–19.

8   See for example J. Kramer, *A Noble Abbot from Mustang: Life and Works of Glo-bo mKhan-chen (1456–1532)*, Wien, 2008, p. 167.

9   Huge images of Maitreya are carved on rocks in the open at Mulbek in lower Ladakh, near Shé in central Ladakh, and at Kartsekar in the Suru Valley; others are fashioned in clay or gilded copper in temples at Alchi, Mangyu, Basgo, and Leh, and one is modelled in concrete in the open, at the monastery of Likir. In southwest Tibet mention should be made of the giant gilded copper Maitreya made by Newar and Tibetan artists in 1914 by order of the Ninth Panchen Lama in a tower-like temple in the monastery of Trashilhünpo.

10   Cf. *The Blue Annals*, ed. G. Roerich and Gendün Chömpel, Varanasi and Delhi, 1976, pp. 1070–71.

11   Cf. Tucci, *Tra giungle e pagode*, pp. 110–11.

12   Cf. the inscription published in E. Lo Bue and F. Ricca, *Gyantse Revisited*, Firenze, 1990, p. 489, n. 275. On the mandalas in this temple see also K. Dowman, "The Mandalas of the Lo Jampa Lhakhang", ed. J. Casey Singer and P. Denwood, *Tibetan Art: Towards a Definition of Style*, London, 1997, pp. 186–95.

13   Cf. Vitali, "On Byams pa and Thub chen lha khang of Glo sMos thang", pp. 17 and 23 n. 15.

14   Cf. D. Jackson, "The Great Western-Himalayan Earthquake of 1505: A

Rupture of the Central Himalayan Gap", *Tibet, Past and Present: Tibetan Studies I, PIATS 2000*, ed. H. Blezer and A. Zadoks, Vol. 2/1, Leiden/Boston/Köln, 2002, pp. 148–59; and *A History of Tibetan Painting: The Great Tibetan Painters and Their Traditions*, Wien, 1996, pp. 77–78 and 80, pl. 2; cf. pp. 81–82.

15   bSod nams rgya mtsho, *The Ngor Mandalas of Tibet: Plates*, Tokyo, 1989, p. x.

16   I thank David Jackson for affording this important bit of information to me (January 8, 2010).

17   See for example Tucci, *Tibetan Painted Scrolls*, p. 103.

18   The king died in 1489. For these respective dates see D. Jackson, *The Mollas of Mustang: Historical, Religious and Oratorical Traditions of the Nepalese-Tibetan Borderland*, Dharamsala, 1984, p. 133; and Bkra shis bstan 'dzin, *Glo ljongs chos kyi zhing sar bstan-pa 'phel rim gyi dkar chag dwangs shel me long*, pp. 110–11 and [284] n. 5, where the author corrects the years given in his text by a cycle of 60.

19   Cf. *Glo ljongs chos kyi zhing sar bstan pa 'phel rim gyi dkar chag dwangs shel me long*, p. [284] n. 5; Vitali, "On Byams pa and Thub chen lha khang of Glo sMos thang", p. 4; and D. Snellgrove and H. Richardson, *A Cultural History of Tibet*, Boulder, 1995, p. 178.

20   E. Lo Bue, "Considerations on the historical and political context of the iconography of three south-western Tibetan temples", *Etudes Tibétaines en l'honneur de Anne Chayet*, ed. J.-L. Achard, Paris, 2010, pp. 147–73. On the cult of Vairochana during the monarchic period see H. Richardson, "The Cult of Vairocana in Early Tibet", *Indo-Tibetan Studies*, ed. T. Skorupski, Tring, 1990, pp. 271–74; and A. Heller, "Early Ninth Century Images of Vairochana from Eastern Tibet", *Orientations*, 25/6, June 1994, pp. 74–78.

21   See for example R. Vitali, *Early Temples of Central Tibet*, London, 1990, pl. 72.

22   Cf. Tucci, *Tra giungle e pagode*, p. 116. Significant changes following the renovation and alteration of the structure of this temple have been discussed by Vitali ("On Byams pa and Thub chen lha khang of Glo sMos thang", pp. 4–6) and by Luigi Fieni in chapter 9. On the meaning of the mural with Vaishravana painted in the ancient vestibule of the Golden Temple at Zhalu see E. Lo Bue, "Chinese Influence in Some Wall Paintings at Zhwa lu and Their Political Meaning within Their Cultural Context", *Gugong Bowuyuan Yuankan (Palace Museum Journal)*, 5/133, 2007, pp. 72–73, and in Jisheng Xie, Wenhua Luo, and Anning Jing, eds., *Studies on Sino-Tibetan Buddhist Art: Proceedings of the Third International Conference of Tibetan Archaeology and Art (Beijing, Capital Normal University, October 13–17, 2006)*, Shanghai, 2009, pp. 217–18, as well as "Considerations on the historical and political context of the iconography of three south-western Tibetan temples".

23   *Lag pa'i 'du byed* and *Pir gyi 'du byed*. For these and other expressions cf. Dhungel, *The Kingdom of Lo (Mustang)*, pp. 239–41, with G. Tucci, *Preliminary Report on Two Scientific Expeditions in Nepal*, Roma, 1956, pp. 16 and 20.

24   The epithet *mi dbang sa yi dbang phyug*, "ruler, lord of the earth", preceding the expression *dpal 'byor bzang po* ("Glorious and Good") may refer to the king's father, the ruler Agön Zangpo. *Mi dbang* is a title used with reference to the king of Gyantsé in an inscription in the temple dedicated to Vairochana in the Great Stupa mentioned above, as well as in the first of a series of eulogies in verses full of Indian imagery and concepts, couched in the "alamkara" style, on the occasion of the completion of the main temple of Gyantsé and reported in the history of its dynasty ('Jigs-med-grags-pa, *rGyal-rtse chos-rgyal-gyi rnam-par-thar-pa dad-pa'i lo-thog dngos-grub-kyi char-'bebs*, Lhasa, 1987, p. 72). However variously edited by Tucci (*Preliminary Report on Two Scientific Expeditions in Nepal*, p. 20) and Dhungel (*The Kingdom of Lo (Mustang)*, p. 250), the part of the inscription referring to the donor clearly reads *tsho dpon bsam me dad pa'i sbyin bdag*, namely "the prefect Sammé, devoted patron", as suggested by David Jackson (personal communication, January 8, 2010). Below, in the same text, a reference to Tsangpa, that is "Brahma", may hint at the name of the founder of the temple, king Tsangchen ("Maha-Brahma") Trashigön.

25   Cf. Tucci, *Preliminary Report on Two Scientific Expeditions in Nepal*, pp. 19–21.

26   Cf. D. Snellgrove, *Four Lamas of Dolpo*, Kathmandu, 1992, pp. 77 and 245.

27   Tucci, *Tra giungle e pagode*, p. 116.

28   See for example Bkra shis bstan 'dzin, *Glo ljongs chos kyi zhing sar bstan pa 'phel rim gyi dkar chag dwangs shel me long*, passim.

CHAPTER 7

Portable Buddhist Sculptures of Lo: A Chronological Selection, 15th through 17th Centuries

Amy Heller

The sanctuaries of Lo abound in sculptures, whether the large-scale clay ones which are an integral part of the architecture, or the smaller, portable images – most often of wood or metal, occasionally ivory – placed on the altars and library shelves. Many of the portable sculptures may have been created elsewhere and subsequently imported into Lo. In order to study works of sculpture which are specifically related to Lo, this article will focus on a small group of Buddhist sculptures comprising portraits of teachers and deities with inscriptions in Tibetan language which describe the circumstances of their casting and/or consecration in Lo. These were all made during the historic period of the dynasty started by Amapel in the early 15th century. The prosperity of this dynasty led to the construction of sanctuaries for the new capital in Lo Möntang, with invitations to artists from afar to embellish them with mural paintings and sculptures, both immovable and portable. The dedicatory inscriptions reveal that the artists were not necessarily natives of Mustang. Frequently they were Newars, probably from the Kathmandu Valley, and there may also have been Tibetan sculptors in the entourage of Tibetan lamas who came to teach in Mustang.

TWO PORTRAITS OF THE FOURTH ABBOT OF NGOR, KÜNGA WANGCHUK (1424–78)

Our earliest examples are two portraits of the fourth abbot of Ngor monastery in southwest Tibet. It has already been established that Künga Zangpo, the founder and first abbot of Ngor, visited Mustang and gave teachings to Amapel and his son (see chapter 1 in this volume). The succeeding abbots of Ngor maintained a close spiritual relationship with the royal family of Lo.[1] It is likely that their portraits too were familiar in the region but are now lost. According to their dedicatory inscriptions, these two sculptures both represent the abbot Künga Wangchuk, and both were made by the same artist, Tsuktorlak. Made of gilt copper, the portraits display similar modelling of body and lotus base, as well as facial physiognomy. Yet they are not identical: one sculpture represents a human teacher, a monk (figures 7.1a and b), while the other is a more altered representation (figures 7.2a and b). Apart from portraying the abbot dressed in monastic robes, he is given the urna, the tuft of hair between the brows which is one of the 33 specific marks of Shakyamuni's divine nature, and a lotus and a book are positioned above the two shoulders, recalling the attributes of Manjushri, the bodhisattva of Wisdom who is regarded as the spiritual ancestor of the Sakya order to which the Ngor abbots belong. Thus the second sculpture is a hypostasis, a representation both divine and human in which the abbot is depicted with divine attributes reflecting his spiritual affinities with Manjushri. The dedicatory inscriptions inform us that both were made at the request of the same donor, Sakyong Ayi Senggé, who was one of the

7.1a and b Portrait of the fourth Ngor abbot as a monk, by the sculptor Tsuktorlak, 1479. Gilt copper, 34 cm. Photographs courtesy of Sotheby's.

sons of Agön Zangpo, Amapel's immediate successor.² These sculptures are therefore a royal commission. They were both made to honour the memory of this abbot, who died in 1478, probably for the ceremony marking the first anniversary of his death. The first paragraph of each dedicatory inscription includes a play on words on the name of Ngorchen Künga Zangpo, whose memory is thus simultaneously honoured by the creation of these sculptures. Künga Wangchuk was a nephew of Ngorchen who presided over his first monastic ordination in 1435 and was his principal teacher. Following in his uncle's footsteps, Wangchuk went to Mustang to teach, then returned to Tibet, where he was named abbot of Ngor in 1465. He returned to Mustang in 1476, and died there. In the official history of the abbatial succession at Ngor, the fourth abbot's biography describes his death in Mustang and the creation of golden statues as part of his funerary and memorial ceremonies there. The statues were subsequently taken to Ngor to honour his memory.

7.2a and b Portrait of the fourth Ngor abbot as a hypostasis of Manjushri, by the sculptor Tsuktorlak, 1479. Gilt copper, 32.5 cm. Photographs courtesy of Sotheby's.

THE ARTIST ABHAYA JYOTI

A very special example is a silver cover of a volume of the Mustang *Kangyur* (a Buddhist canonical text), with carved Buddhas and emblems, which bears a dedicatory inscription attributing it to a specific sculptor working as part of a team. This book cover (figure 7.3) is a wonder of miniature carving in silver repoussé with parcel gilding of details. Along the upper edge are ten Buddhas, seated in the meditative posture (vajraparyankasana), and displaying the dharmachakra mudra of teaching, literally "setting the wheel of the Dharma in motion". These Buddhas are all wearing monastic garments. They have no jewellery, their hair is in short curls, and they are barefoot. Their appearance corresponds to that of Shakyamuni Buddha, the Buddha in human body (nirmanakaya). These ten Buddhas are probably to be understood as representing the Buddhas of the Ten Fields, corresponding to the cardinal points, the intermediary points, and the zenith and nadir of the universe, a reminder of Shakyamuni whose teachings spread in all directions. On either side of the group of Buddhas is a hole for a nail to attach this silver repoussé to its wooden backing. Four seated male deities are aligned vertically on each side panel. These are the Eight Bodhisattvas (lit.: the beings destined for enlightenment) who are represented in the body of bliss (sambhogakaya), wearing royal garments of shawl and dhoti, and royal jewellery of earrings and necklaces. They are all seated cross-legged, in vajrasana. Each holds the hands in a different position to display their distinguishing attributes or emblems, not all of which can be discerned. At the centre, in relief with gilding, we see in the large letters of the Tibetan Uchen alphabet, the expression "in the language of India" ("*Gyagar kè du*"), which is the standard opening stanza for a Buddhist scripture translated into Tibetan. The title of the text is given first in the original Sanskrit, and then in Tibetan transliteration.

In smaller letters of incised carving in Tibetan, there is a dedicatory inscription. It informs us that the scribe of the volume was a man named Sanggyèpel of Tingkhyu, which is a village in northern Dölpo, the region west of Mustang which was also culturally and ethnically Tibetan. The principal sculptor is named: the glorious artist the Newar Abhaya Jyoti ("A pha Dza ti" in the inscription), who worked on this cover with others. He was thus the foreman of a team of artisans working on this cover and on those of the remaining volumes in the series.[3] Thanks to a volume from the same series in the library of the royal palace of Lo, we can understand how this silver plate was originally inserted as the central section of the inner face of the wooden bookcover (figure 7.4). Here we see the central

7.3 Cover of a volume of the Mustang *Kangyur*, by the sculptor Abhaya Jyoti and others, 1511. Silver, 15.5 x 41.5 cm. Private collection.

7.4 Cover of a volume of the Mustang *Kangyur* in the Raja's personal chapel, by the sculptors Abhaya Jyoti and Rup Tej, 1511. Silver with gold letters, 20 x 67 cm. Photograph: Thomas Laird 1992.

section identical to the previous example, but in this case it is flanked by an enshrined Shakyamuni at left and an enshrined Avalokiteshvara at right. Here, too there is a dedicatory inscription of blessings, stating that these excellent examples of the Buddhist deities and the raised gold letters are the mark of the Newar master craftsmen Rup Tej (in the inscription, "Ru pa te dza") [and Abhaya Jyoti], father and son.[4] In fact, the last page of the book clarifies the identification of these two sculptors. The book was made in 1511, the work of the Shakya-bhikshu Rup Tej and his son Abhaya Jyoti, both of Mimmanani Bahal in Kathmandu, during the reign of Ratna Malla. These Shakya-bhikshus also belonged to Manjushri Naka Mahavihara.[5] In addition to the manuscript, silver utensils, tangkas, and other requirements for the temple of Jampa at Möntang were supplied by the Shakya-bhikshu father and son.[6]

Another work by Abhaya Jyoti is a statue representing the bodhisattva Avalokiteshvara, dated by inscription to 1543, cast in a non-gilt copper alloy (figure 7.5). The letters of the Tibetan text are incised all along the base of the sculpture. The text reads, "To honour the memory of Pema Wangyel [who is one with] the omniscient Avalokiteshvara, best god of gods, [the donor] Zangpo Lhajin had this [image] completed with deep reverence and faith by the skilled Newar Abhaya Jyoti [Apha Jyoti or Jayati] on the 15th day of the first month of the water-female-sheep year. By virtue [of making this image] may all beings rapidly attain Buddhahood. Blessings."[7]

Avalokiteshvara is the bodhisattva of Compassion. Here he is clasping the stem of a lotus which blooms above his left shoulder. His right hand is extended in the gesture of bestowing a gift, because this is the special aspect of Avalokiteshvara who bestows the boon of ensuring release from

Buddhist hells. He is called Chittavishramana Avalokiteshvara, namely "Avalokiteshvara (who sets) the Mind at Ease". This aspect is associated with a group of texts that teach how to eliminate suffering by ensuring release from Buddhist hells. The Buddhist doctrine teaches that if a person has been evil, he or she may be reborn in the hells, which is one of the six realms of existence: those of heavenly beings, demigods, human beings, animals, hungry ghosts, and hell beings, respectively. The choice of this form of Avalokiteshvara thus links this artistic representation to the after-death period.

In fact, according to the inscription carved in Tibetan letters along the base of the image, this statue is a representation of the Nyingmapa teacher Ngari Panchen Pema Wangyel (1487–1542) as Avalokiteshvara, due to the Ngari Panchen's great spirituality. The inscription furthermore states that this is a funerary image, made in homage to the lama after his death for the spiritual benefit of all sentient beings, and cast by Abhaya Jyoti, the skilled Newari artist named in the inscription. The teachings of the Ngari Panchen were deemed to be so effective for those who heard them that release from suffering was similar to that obtained by veneration of Avalokiteshvara. Thus, upon his death, the teacher was represented in the ideal body of the bodhisattva. This image illustrates the hypostasis of the lama as a bodhisattva, similar to the statue of the fourth abbot of Ngor (figures 7.2a and b).

7.5a and b Portrait of Ngari Panchen Pema Wangyel as an aspect of Avalokiteshvara, by the sculptor Abhaya Jyoti, 1543. Non-gilt copper alloy, 16.5 cm. Asia Society, New York, gift from The Blanchette Hooker Rockefeller Fund, Acc. no. 1994.004.

It is typical for an image to be made for the special ceremony marking the one-year death anniversary of a high lama. As there are very few teachers named Pema Wangyel, it is quite likely that this image was made in 1543, one year after Pema Wangyel's death. Although 1543 is a water-female-hare year in the Tibetan calendar, the scribe has written "a water-female-sheep year". This is likely to be an error in copying, as such scribal errors are not infrequent. In view of the other works of art by Abhaya Jyoti, and in view of the birth of the Ngari Panchen in northern Lo, near the Lo Gekar monastery, it is quite possible that this image was also made in Lo. As a child, he studied religion locally under the guidance of his father, an accomplished teacher, and then studied also with the royal scion Lowo Khenchen Sönam Lhündrup, from whom he received full monastic ordination at the age of 25. He went to Dölpo shortly after, to meditate at the sacred mountain Shé, then he travelled widely in Tibet as well as to Kathmandu. The donor of the sculpture, Zangpo Lhajin, has an ethnic Tibetan name, but we do not know where he lived. He may have been a Tibetan or a native of Mustang.[8]

Although the Ngari Panchen died in Tibet, due to his fame as a teacher in Mustang it is probable that this memorial image was sculpted in his native land. The identification of the artist is clear, but whether he was working in Kathmandu or in Mustang to make this sculpture remains unknown. His virtuosity is remarkable, and it is hoped that future research will bring to light other images from the hands of this artist.

TWO ROYAL PORTRAITS OF THE GREAT ABBOT OF LO, SÖNAM LHÜNDRUP (1456–1532)

Our next examples are two sculptures representing the prince Sönam Lhündrup. A renowned monk in the Sakya order, he became the Great Abbot of Lo. He occupied a significant position as a teacher, a writer, and a political statesman. The long inscription on the base of the first sculpture (figure 7.6) indicates that this portrait was probably made as a funerary image to honour his memory by family members. The sculptor is named in the inscription as Namkhadrak. This is historically identified as the name of a distinguished artist who is known to have worked at Khojarnath in 1512 sculpting numerous clay statues. It is probable that the image of Sönam Lhündrup is the work of this sculptor.[9]

This sculpture is in non-gilt copper alloy, with silver and red copper inlay. It is a very commanding image, due to the steadfast gaze and stern expression of the face. It is also lavish in the decoration of the monastic robes. The inner robe has edges of alternating red copper and silver engraving of floral motifs while the hem of the robe is engraved with the eight auspicious emblems of Buddhism. Even the fingernails are enhanced with copper inlay. The feet, hands, and face are all painted in gold. While it is common for a portrait to have pigment for the hair and eyes, and matte gold for the face, the use of brilliant gold such as here is highly unusual. There is a genuine sense of portraiture in comparison with other inscribed images of

Opposite
7.6 Portrait of the Great Abbot of Lo, by the sculptor Namkhadrak, 1533. Non-gilt copper alloy, silver and copper inlay, 29.2 cm. Photograph courtesy of Sotheby's.

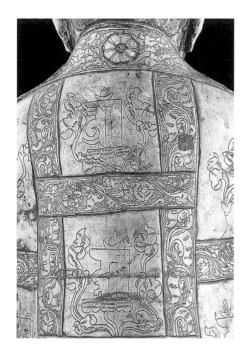

7.7a and b Portrait of the Great Abbot of Lo, 1533(?). Non-gilt copper alloy, silver and copper inlay, 44 cm. Photographs courtesy of Rossi and Rossi (7a); Seer Gallery, Beijing (7b).

the Great Abbot as well as with our next example, which is not inscribed, but unmistakably depicts the same subject (figures 7.7a and b).

This superb sculpture is an exceptionally large cast metal portrait. The physiognomy is remarkably similar to the previous one despite the difference in scale. Again there is silver and copper inlay to enhance the face, silver for the eyes and copper for the lips. The monastic robes are also embellished with flowers, clouds, and auspicious emblems in silver and copper. On the robe at the back of the image the syllable "om" is delicately incised in the Lantsa alphabet (figure 7.7b). While there is no inscription, the large scale of the sculpture and its lavish ornamentation tend to indicate that this was made as a funerary offering to honour the memory of this great statesman and teacher.

SUCCEEDING GENERATIONS OF THE ROYAL FAMILY OF LO AS PATRONS OF THE ARTS

As our next examples, we will examine two statues linked with the ninth generation of the royal family of Lo, the 17th-century religious king Agön Samdrup Rapten and his family. First, we examine a sculpture of a Buddha and its prabhamandala, literally "circle of glory", the elaborate oval backrest cum aureole of the sculpture (figure 7.8). Here, the viewer initially apprehends a c. 8th–9th-century Kashmiri or Gilgit sculpture of a seated Buddha on his throne. The Buddha is represented according to the classical aesthetic mode of that period, yet the face has the matte gold paint and pigments indicative of Tibetan consecration practices. The sculpture of the Buddha is gilt which also is not characteristic of sculptures made in Kashmir or Gilgit. Further observation reveals that the prabhamandala is finely worked in gilt copper repoussé and corresponds to Nepalese models with a Garuda at the apex. At the base of the throne, there is a carefully carved inscription in Tibetan letters. Indeed the inscription informs us that in 1663–64, to commemorate the death of the Lo ruler Agön Samdrup Rapten, the lady Nyida and her children commissioned the Nepalese sculptor Surya Jyoti to sculpt the exquisite torana frame to adorn this most precious statue of the Buddha as it was reconsecrated for the benefit of all sentient beings. This sculpture, therefore, represents a unique juncture of two aesthetic modes as a result of Buddhist ritual practices to revere an ancient statue and thus renew its spirituality.

The identification of the donor has been somewhat problematic. Agön Samdrup Rapten's granddaughter was known as Nyida Wangmo,[10] while his wife was known as Nyida Gyelmo.[11] Agön Samdrup Rapten and his wife were active sponsors of Buddhist sculptures, religious texts, and stupas, according to local Mustang historical records.[12] It is therefore more likely that the donor was his wife. The height of the Buddha statue as originally cast on its lion base is 47 centimetres, while the total height of the prabha added in c. 1663–64, is 67 centimetres (from the ground to the apex of the prabha). The seated Buddha itself measures 29 centimetres, and is cast in brass alloy, but during the subsequent consecration in 1663–64, the

7.8 Buddha Shakyamuni
enshrined in his
prabhamandala. Shakyamuni,
Kashmir or Gilgit, c.
725–750. Gilt brass alloy and
pigments, 47 cm.
Prabhamandala for
Shakyamuni, by the sculptor
Surya Jyoti, 1663–64. Gilt
copper repoussé, 67 cm.
Pritzker Collection.
Photograph: Hughes Dubois.

sculpture was gilded and matte gold and pigments were applied to the face and hair. The unusual montage of Kashmiri and Newar aesthetic models allows us to understand the appreciation of both at the Mustang court. They culminate as a new aesthetic form, an expression of the unique eclecticism characteristic of Tibetan sculpture.[13]

Our second example linked to this king and his wife is a portrait of a lama which they commissioned as a memorial to him shortly after his death (figures 7.9a and b). The long dedicatory inscription names the lama and describes the rulers' joint sponsorship of this statue in the hope of long life, good health, continuity of their political power, wealth, and the prosperity of the kingdom.[14] The statue is a realistic portrait of Lama Chögyel Püntsok, with very individualistic features and facial hair, such as the narrow moustache and goatee, as well as the long hair piled into a high braided

7.9a and b Portrait of Lama Chögyel Püntsok, c. 1650. Gilt copper and pigments, 67 cm. Private collection. Photographs: Amy Heller.

chignon above his low headgear. The lama wears religious garments with very intricately carved floral designs. The statue is elegant testimony to the eminence of this lama who is known to have served as the rulers' personal chaplain according to a historical text, the *Tsarang Molla*.[15]

Our final example is the funerary portrait of Lama Püntsok Sherap (figure 7.10), the personal chaplain of Samdrup Pembar, the second son of Agön Samdrup Rapten who succeeded him as religious king in the last quarter of the 17th century. Püntsok Sherap was born in Tibet but he migrated to Lo where he served as chief preceptor to this king who "sponsored the making of inconceivably many sacred images, books, and stupas".[16] This portrait again is a very realistic rendition of the lama's physiognomy and appearance, especially the high chignon and non-monastic religious robes. The lama has a turquoise between his brows, to represent the urna, and he holds a vase of long life. According to the inscription, the image is made in homage to the memory of "Vajradhara Mipam Püntsok Sherap", the prefix Vajradhara clearly indicating that in this portrait, the lama is represented as a Buddha.[17]

***

To conclude, in the small group of sculptures examined here, the dedicatory inscriptions reveal the name of the subject, the date of the commission, the name and status of some donors, and even the artists' names, often in relation with the royal family of Lo. These few examples have given us an opportunity to observe the variety of sculptures appreciated in the kingdom of Lo, in small and large scale, the techniques of cast and repoussé sculpture, the use of silver, gilt copper, and non-gilt copper alloys, with silver, copper, and turquoise inlay. The sculptors excelled in portraying lifelike physiognomies and in conveying a strong sense of spirituality and reverence towards the doctrines and teachers of Buddhism.

NOTES

1   According to the Historical Succession of the Abbots of Ngor (Sangs rgyas phun tshogs, *Ngor gdan rabs nor bu 'phreng ba*, Dehradun, 1985, pp. 6–11).

2   See D. Jackson, *The Mollas of Mustang*, Dharamsala, 1984, pp. 120, 124, 133; R.K. Dhungel, *The Kingdom of Lo (Mustang)*, Kathmandu, 2002, pp. 93–95. At the time these were made in 1479, the ruler was Trashigön, Ayi Senggé's brother. That is why Ayi Senggé has the title Sakyong which is indicative of his aristocratic status. After Trashigön's death in 1489, he participated more actively in the government.

3   The inscription reads: *Yi ge pa ni Ting khyu Sangs rgyas/ dpal 'phrul byed Ne dpal A pa dza ti sogs/ zhang tshan gsum dang dza rag rnams kyi sgrubs/ sbyin bdag phu phag Rdo rje tshe dbang lags/ mangalam//.*

4   The inscription reads: *Om svasti siddham/ mtshan dpes rab mdzes rgyal ba'i sku/ gser 'od 'bar ba'i yi ge 'bru'i gzugs// ru pa te dza pha bu sogs// bal yul mkhas pa'i sug rjes lags//.* I thank the Venerable Tsenshap Rinpoché (Zurich) for the interpretation of *sug rjes* as "seal"/"mark", in relation to the Tibetan terms *sug byang* "seal" and *lag rjes* "finger-print". I am indebted to Gautama Vajracharya for the information that *jyoti = dpal* = "brilliance". It is a Newar name, particularly common among the Uda (Urha) caste. I thank Erberto Lo Bue for the information that this name is also found among Newar artists of the Shakya-bhikshu caste, such as the most famous sculptor of the 20th century, Man Jyoti Shakya, his father Pancha Jyoti, brother Tej Jyoti, and son Ratna Jyoti.

5   I am grateful to Corneille Jest for sending me the translation of research by

Opposite

7.10 Portrait of Lama Püntsok Sherap, late 17th–early 18th century. Gilt copper and pigments, turquoise inlay, 52 cm. San Antonio Museum of Art, purchased with funds provided by the Ewing Halsell Foundation, 2004.7.1. Photograph: Peggy Tenison.

Harsha Muni Shakya (now deceased, formerly of Lagan Tole, Kathmandu), published in *Pragati Quarterly*, 2/1, January 2004, pp. 1–2, "The contribution of Shakya Bhikshu Ruptejpal in the Development of the Kingdom of Blo". Both these monasteries, Mimmanani Bahal and Manjushri Naka Mahavihara, are located in the southern section of old Kathmandu city.

6   Harsha Muni Shakya, ibid.

7   I thank Ven. Tsenshap Rinpoché, Karma Puntso, and Dan Martin for their criticism of my translation and thank the Asia Society for kindly providing photographs. Inscription along base: *//Om sva sti/ kun mkhyen lha'i lha mchog spyan ras gzigs// padma dbang rgyal dgongs pa rdzogs phyir tu// bzang po lha sbyin rab gus dad pa yis// cho mo lug gi cho 'phrul dus chen la// ne bal mkhas pa a pha jayatis bsgrubs// dge bas 'gro kun sangs rgyas myur thob shog// mangalam//.* This mahapandita is mentioned in chapter 1 as Pema Wangyel Dorjé.

8   The donor has not yet been identified. This statue was first published in 1975, but its historical significance was misunderstood. See U. von Schroeder, *Indo-Tibetan Bronzes*, Hong Kong, 1981, plate 133b, citing Sotheby's catalogue of September 18, 1975, item 359.

9   See R. Vitali, "Introduction" to Wagindrakarma, *The Historical Record of the Three Silver Brothers of Khojarnath (Jo bo rin po che dngul sku mched gsum rten dang brten par bcas pa'i dkar chag rab dga'i glu dbyangs)*, Dharamsala, 1996, p. 13.

10   Dhungel, *The Kingdom of Lo (Mustang)*, p. 111.

11   According to the royal genealogy of Mustang, compiled by the lama bCo brgyad Khri chen, cited by Dhungel, *The Kingdom of Lo (Mustang)*, p. 104.

12   *Tsarang Molla*, f. 12a, cited by Dhungel, *The Kingdom of Lo (Mustang)*, pp. 104–05.

13   **Inscription:**
Om svasti/ rmad byung tshogs gnyis chu gter dbus su'khrungs/ rnam dag byang chub spyod pa'i khams las grub// 'phags sras gser ri'i dbus na nyer mdzes pa// thub dbang rinchen rdul brtsegs la phyag 'tshal// chos dpal chen 'am mgonbsam 'grub rab brtan gyi thugs kyi dgongs pa yongsu rdzogspar gyur zhing/ bdag nyi zla ma bu 'khor dang bcas pa lamchog thun mong gi dngos grub ma lus pa brtsal du gsol// bzorig bal po bzo su dza 'dzo tri sogs dbang po 'grangs can kyis sgrubs// bkra shis//

     Translation:

Om Svasti.

To honour the memory* of the glorious Ah mgon bSam grub rab brtan, in the hopes that Nyi Zla mother and child(ren) and all sentient beings may attain the superior and the mundane levels of spiritual realization, the Nepalese workmanship (i.e. the creation of the prabha) is the achievement of the master artist Su Dza dzo ti,** the sculptor of infinite prowess.

May there be praise to the Buddha who is most precious,*** (he who is) the noble son in the centre of the golden mountain of beautiful offerings, he who has totally perfected the practices leading to enlightenment as the result of the karma of birth in the centre of the ocean combining the two excellent conditions (= wealth and religion, i.e. Shakyamuni Buddha was born as Prince Siddhartha and he had religious aspirations). May there be happiness!

     Notes:

* Literally, "to fulfil completely the intentions or spiritual aspirations", in analogy to the Buddha, whose death was his mahaparinirvana. Thus this is an idiomatic expression, it means "to die". When an image is made in complete fulfilment of the person's intentions, it means that it was made soon after the person's death, usually for the one-year commemorative ceremony.

** Gautama Vajracharya suggests this is a transliteration of Surya Jyoti, a common Newar name, particularly for Udas, while Erberto Lo Bue suggests that it refers to the Shakya-bhikshus. The three Newar castes among which metal sculptors are still to be found are the Vajracharya, Shakya, and Uda according to E. Lo Bue, "Casting of Devotional Images in the Himalayas: history, tradition and modern techniques", in W. Oddy and W. Zwalf, *Aspects of Tibetan Metallurgy*, London, 1981, p. 70. Dan Martin suggested the possibility of reading Sujana Jyoti as the sculptor's name. My thanks to all of them.

*** Literally, "the mighty sage of precious particles all piled up together".

14   Excerpt from the translation of the inscription: "... To honour the memory of the glorious lama and in the hope of the blessings of long life, good health, continuity of political power, wealth and prosperity for ourselves and the inhabitants of the kingdom."

Text of the inscription:

Na mo gu ru/ phun tshogs dge legs kun'byung thod phreng rtsal (bstal) skal ldan don du shag rigs bod rjer sprul// zab gter dam chos srid 'dzin zad de'i sku// dad ldan 'dod dgu 'byung ba 'di zhengs pas// dpal ldan bla ma'i thugs dgongs rdzogs pa dang/ bdag srogs 'khor bcas tshe ring nad med cing// mnga' thang dpal 'byor phan (phun) tshogs dam chos ldan/ bsam don 'grub cing 'di phyu kun tu skyobs/ a ma rigs skye a' mgon dang lha lcam nyi zla'i zhengs// ma ma a yur pu nya shri bhu ti gu na sar va va lda gu ru/ ma ha ka ru no ka pa'i gu ru/ a dhi shadra a nantu/ mangalam//

15   See Jackson, pp. 150, 155.

16   *Tsarang Molla*, cited and translated by Jackson, p. 150 for discussion of the religious king Samdrup Pembar and his teacher Mipam Püntsok Sherap.

17   "Homage and reverence to the noble Vajradhara Mipam Püntsok Sherap, by me, Püntsok Tsünmo Jangchup tsomo. May this saint's aspirations be fulfilled." // *rje btsun rdo rje 'chang mi pham phun tshogs shes rab la bdag phun tshogs byang chub mtsho mo phyag 'tshal zhing skyabsu mchi/ dam pa de nyid kyi thugs dgongs rdzogs//*

RESTORATION
AND REVIVAL

CHAPTER 8

The Restoration of Murals
in the Maitreya Temple of Möntang

Luigi Fieni

The Maitreya temple (Jampa Lhakhang) was the first religious building constructed in Möntang (figure 8.1). Its exceedingly complex history, combined with many unanswered questions, casts an aura of mystery on the temple. Its date of completion is one of its first ambiguities, as no records have been found to establish reliable dating. Some scholars attribute the completion date to Lama Ngorchen Künga Zangpo's[1] last visit to Lo, but that is a debatable conclusion for the temple has never been completed, as will be explained later. Most probably Ngorchen's last visit consisted simply in the consecration of the temple shrine, which did not at all signify the completion of the work.

The temple rises 17 metres above the ground floor from a large courtyard containing 18 (of the original 20) pillars. Some traces of stuccowork on the pillars suggest that at one time they were all decorated in stucco. The temple's rammed-mud walls, nearly 1.6 metres thick at the base, form two levels, each finely painted. Each storey had a corridor, but only one is still present: the upper one probably collapsed during the 16th-century earthquake, leaving only a portion still visible. It appears that a small area of the corridor wall on the south side was once painted, as there is some flaking on its surface typical of a paint layer. Unfortunately the conditions of preservation are so poor that it is impossible to prove this assertion. A third storey, added and painted much later,[2] was built with sun-baked mud brick.

The organization of the pictorial cycle is quite complex.

The ground floor corridor was meant to be painted on both sides. At present there are paintings on almost all the inner walls as well as some remnants of paint on the outer walls on the south and west sides. A great portion of the west wall has collapsed, along with the whole northern outer wall. More recently, to combat the rising dampness that had eroded the whole lower section, the local community built a new mud-rammed wall and a buttressing stone wall. No traces of paintings are left on the northern outer wall.

As for the murals on the inner walls, the southern and northern sides depict five huge deities surrounded by hundreds of images of the Buddha Amitayus (figure 8.2). The western side is severely damaged, yet the five deities are still visible. Buddha is placed at the centre, precisely on the vertical axis of the Maitreya statue in the second storey. The east wall is a case of its own. One finds four Buddhas with two attendants depicted in relief work known as pastiglia, a technique present only on that one wall of the monastery (figure 8.3). This different style of painting might suggest that this wall was painted much later,[3] perhaps during or after the execution of the Mahamuni temple. The pastiglia technique is widely employed in the Mahamuni temple murals; thus, it seems possible that the artists who worked there influenced the painters working in the Maitreya temple. Interestingly,

8.1 Maitreya temple, first floor terrace and upper portion, 15th century.

the faces and bodies of two of those four Buddhas were scratched off. At first this seemed to be the result of vandalism, but later it was found that the local Tibetan doctor (*amchi*) had scraped off the sacred paint on purpose in order to mix it with medicinal herbs to be used in the attempt to cure severe illnesses. In the lower area, episodes from the life of Buddha are painted, but not completed. Interestingly, preparatory sketches are still visible along with single letters or numbers used as colour indicators.

The remains on the outer walls depict five gigantic images, four of them being wrathful divinities, with a Buddha at the centre. All the divinities are surrounded by the five transcendental Buddhas distinguished by their respective gestures (figure 8.4). Above two narrow windows at the southwest corner, two minor deities are depicted, suggesting that each corner once had two different characters; unfortunately, no other traces are left.

8.2 Sitatapatra surrounded by Amitayus Buddhas, by Gyeltsen from Gungtang. Maitreya temple, ground floor circumambulation corridor, inner wall, south, 15th century. Distemper.

8.3 Detail of the east wall before restoration. Maitreya temple, ground floor, 15th century. Distemper.

The first floor once hosted a sequence of 54 mandalas, dedicated to peaceful and wrathful deities. At present only 47 are clearly visible. The sequence is based on 12 large mandalas enclosing five smaller ones on the south and north walls (figure 8.5). There are just four large mandalas on the west wall with an empty space between them and the statue of Maitreya. That space was never meant to be painted, for a very small portion of a painted textile, in the same style and quality of the murals, demonstrates that two huge tangkas once hung on both sides of the Maitreya statue. The east wall hosts 12 large mandalas enclosing four smaller ones and a series of 11 guardians protecting the entrance door. Flower decorations and minor deities surround the mandalas on each of the painted walls.

8.5 Mandalas after restoration. Maitreya temple, first floor, southeast corner, 15th century. Distemper.

Opposite
8.4 Parnashavari surrounded by the five transcendental Buddhas. Maitreya temple, ground floor circumambulation corridor, outer wall, south, 15th century. Distemper.

The second floor contains mandalas of a tantric nature (figure 8.6). Entry to this floor has for years been forbidden to all foreigners after a renowned photographer attempted to clean the murals so as to take better pictures, and ended up washing away portions of the 15th-century paintings. Only after several years of assiduous efforts in restoring the temple of Mahamuni were we granted access to work on the murals in the temple of Maitreya. At present, 42 mandalas remain, at least partially. Given the serious state of degradation on the north wall, it is difficult to ascertain the original number of mandalas. Leakage from the ceiling has nearly washed away many of the paintings, with the exception of a few mandalas. Traces of a guardian, set unusually to the north side, establish the location of the entrance door. The deities and lamas that surround the mandalas are painted in a style quite distinct from those on the first floor, thereby suggesting a different period of execution.

The diversity of stratifications found in the wall paintings of the Maitreya temple suggests that many different techniques were used to prepare the walls for painting. The number of preparatory layers varies from floor to floor, and on the ground floor almost every wall has a different stratification. It is very important indeed to know the exact number of preparatory layers as such information can yield precious clues about the period of painting as well as the painters. In fact, the number of layers varies from period to period. One may assume that masters working contemporaneously would have used the same technique to prepare the walls because they would have employed the same masons to prepare the plasters. The fact that three methods of stratification are found on the ground floor proves that there were several masters, each with his own style,[4] working at different times.

In contrast, the first floor has two extremely homogeneous preparatory layers applied on a rammed-mud-based wall. The thickness of the first layer is approximately 1.3 centimetres and the material is composed of a mixture of clay, cow dung, and vegetal fibres. The cow dung is employed so as to

8.6 Mandala after restoration. Maitreya temple, second floor, south wall, 15th century. Distemper.

increase the adhesive properties of the mixture, while the vegetal fibres form a skeleton that strengthens the plaster.

The second layer, much finer in granulometry, measures just 7 millimetres and is composed of clay and very fine vegetal fibres bound together with excreta. This mixture results in a very flat surface. A white coating of kaolin and gypsum mixed with animal glue is then applied as a priming layer. All brushstrokes are visible in raking light.

On each floor, prior to making the preparatory drawing on the final layer, an artist's space was prepared with a highly complex grid of directional lines executed with the aid of a snapping cord embedded in red or black ink. The preparatory drawing is a thick sketch, carried out with bamboo sticks used as pens, including letters or numbers to indicate the intended colour pattern. In this way, each area to be painted in the same colour would be marked with the same sign. A coat of shellac was applied on top of the preparatory drawing, probably to keep the drawing from disappearing as it was painted. Given that all the preparatory layers were water-sensitive and the binder of the paint was water-based, this protective layer was essential. Moreover, the shellac would prevent colour from being absorbed by the porous surface of the walls.

Using an infrared camera, an interesting example of an intricate grid has been found on the inner south wall of the ground floor. The grid is traversed by diagonals whose intersections have been used as centres to

8.7 Infrared image showing preparatory drawing. Maitreya temple, ground floor, south corridor, 15th century.

draw a sequence of small Buddha images (figure 8.7). They are enclosed in circles drawn using compasses (or stringed nails) and, by raking light, their engraved centres remain clearly visible in each figure.

Guided by the letters and numbers, the paint layer was finally applied. The pigments used by the artists were the traditional ones, and, after the murals had been cleaned, we found a very rich palette on all three floors:[5] cinnabar for red, orpiment for yellow, malachite or orpiment mixed with carbon black for green, and azurite or indigo for blue. White was obtained from a mixture of calcite, gypsum, and kaolin. Each colour used animal glue as its binder. Shading was executed using transparent layers of different lacquers. In addition, powdered gold was applied with a binder to create intricate jewellery and delicate patterns on the deities' garments as well as the ornamentation on the mandalas. An impressive use of glossy black-ink outlines of varying thicknesses delineates the mandalas, deities, and flowers thus giving the paintings extraordinary elegance.

The ground floor shows evidence that it was never completed. The walls of the main shrine, containing a gigantic clay image of Maitreya, were not painted.[6] However, traces of construction lines snapped with a cord

8.8 Detail showing a blue background with two different hues of indigo. Maitreya temple, first floor, south wall, 15th century. Distemper.

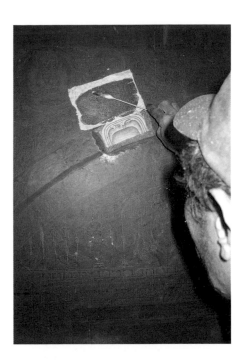

8.9 Cleaned sample showing the brilliance of the original colours. Maitreya temple, first floor, east wall. Distemper.

soaked in red colour and a few sketch-lines found randomly prove that, for unknown reasons, the pictorial cycle on the ground floor was never started. Furthermore, parts of the wall paintings – including the sky, as well as some figures and gilded refinements – are missing from the circumambulation corridor surrounding the main shrine. In addition, a few areas show just the priming layer without any trace of colour. Numbers used to mark which colours should be applied are still visible in some of the figures within those areas, as the figures remain entirely unpainted. It may be that the painters ran out of funds after the initial work because of the cost of the wars fought by Lo against Purang and Gugé.[7]

The most engaging colour on the first floor is the blue of the sky, with different hues of indigo clearly defined by square and rectangular areas enclosing one or more mandalas. The various hues of blue depend on the different proportions of indigo and carbon black or cinnabar. Since the space was divided into sections, we may surmise that the blues were prepared on different days or by different artists (figure 8.8). It is difficult to say whether it was the same painter who painted the sections on different days or if more painters were involved at one particular time. The only evident stylistic difference is noted in the execution of the west wall, where an inscription proves the painter's Newar origin. This wall is also the most refined painting on the floor.[8] Doubtless, the master would have drawn the figures, marking with letters and numbers the colours that his students were to apply. The finishing of the paintings, such as the shading and the application of gold, was more likely executed by the master, for it is a work of great skill and precision.

Thanks to these clues, it is possible to infer that the wall paintings on the first floor were completed before those on the ground floor. Only later was the second floor added. The shrine of a Tibetan temple must be painted before any other storey because it contains the temple's main devotional image. This practice is similar to the Christian tradition in which the apse is the first section of a new church to be painted so that people can start worshipping the main image even though the structure is not yet completed.

As for the state of preservation, the temple was in fragile condition. At all four corners, the walls were separated from each other by several centimetres for the full height of the temple. A dreadful situation was found on the first storey of the temple. As mentioned above, the murals of this floor were painted on top of two preparatory clay-based plaster layers. On the southern and western walls more than 60 square metres of the upper layer, on which the murals were painted, had become detached a few centimetres from the lower layer, thereby creating a high risk of collapse. Moreover, serious rain infiltrations from the ceiling had washed away several sections of the paint layer on all the storeys, as its binder was water-sensitive and its plaster/varnish water-soluble. On the ground floor, heavy leakage of water and clay from the ceiling had covered most of the pictorial cycle with a thick muddy coating. The upper storey was another difficult case indeed, as sunlight from an opening in the ceiling had altered a good portion of the

murals. Moreover, water infiltrations had washed away many paint layers on the west and north walls.

    The fixing of the flaking paint layer and the reattachment of the preparatory layers were the first operations undertaken in a process that took four work seasons. The paint flakes were first thoroughly cleaned of dust and subsequently unrolled back into position using special spatulas and organic binders purposely designed and tested for this restoration. The spaces between preparatory layers were filled with a gluing solution composed of the same clays used in the original technique.

    In the case of the ground floor of the Maitreya temple, the thick coating of mud was removed using surgical scalpels and glass-fibre pencils. This was an extraordinarily difficult task for it had to be performed without harming or abrading the paint layer, working millimetre by millimetre for the entire surface of the walls.

    The precarious situation on the second storey of the Maitreya temple required very careful interventions: the paintings were so far separated from the first layer that the weight of an anchoring mixture to fill the gap might have caused the wall's collapse and the loss of priceless paintings; thus, the gap had to be reduced prior to the insertion of the anchoring mixture. To accomplish this task, specially produced stop-drill bits from Italy were inserted into the pictorial layer, thereby creating a kind of grid attaching the painting securely to the wall. Day by day, the gradual tightening of the drill-

8.10 Local restorers toning down light spots and balancing hues. Maitreya temple, first floor, south wall.

bits reduced the separation of the two surfaces so that the void was finally narrow enough to be filled without risk. In this way, we were eventually able to inject an anchoring mixture to secure the wall paintings; only after this process could we inject the gluing solution.

The next challenging step required the cleaning of the wall paintings, a risky operation, since the use of unsuitable chemicals could irreversibly damage the pictorial layer. Tests were carried out in situ and, with the aid of laboratory analysis, we successfully removed the altered varnish and alien deposits from the surface of the paintings.

In general, the cleaning process was exceedingly challenging because the binder of the paint layer was as water-soluble as the varnish. So as to

8.11 The main statue of Maitreya after restoration. Maitreya temple, throne on the ground floor and statue on the first floor, west wall, 1663. Painted clay.

prevent possible damage, all cleaning operations were carried out with the aid of a special Japanese tissue paper applied between the paint layer and the chemical. By patiently applying the chemicals through the tissue paper, it was possible to remove the varnish while preserving the original paint layer from dissolution (figure 8.9).

Once the cleaning was complete, our efforts turned to plastering. The purpose of this operation was to fill any lacunae, thereby returning an optical equilibrium to the mural's paint layer. Small losses that could be reconstructed were plastered up to the level of the paint layer, while wider ones were plastered under the level of the paint imitating the colour and roughness of the original preparatory layers.

An appropriate set of lightproof watercolours was used to tone down or balance the surface and the abrasions of the wall paintings (figure 8.10), while natural pigments were chosen for the reconstruction that took place in

8.12 Detail of mandala after restoration. Maitreya temple, first floor, east wall, 15th century. Distemper.

the few areas where it was possible. To avoid reconstructive misinterpretation, the larger lacunae were left slightly under the level of the paint layer using a plaster imitating the original one.

The restoration process also included the repair of all statues and chortens within the temple, including the statue of Maitreya[9] (figure 8.11).

Though our work continues, a visitor to the Maitreya temple is now able to experience the murals much as a 15th-century viewer might have, enjoying the shrine's powerful and meaningful images depicted in colours returned to their original brightness (figure 8.12).

FIGURE ACKNOWLEDGEMENTS
All photographs by Luigi Fieni.

NOTES

1   K. Dowman ("The Mandalas of the Lo Jampa Lhakhang", *Tibetan Art: Towards a definition of style*, ed. J. Casey Singer and P. Denwood, London, 1997, p. 189) states that the Maitreya temple was completed between Ngorchen Künga Zangpo's last two visits to Lo, between 1424 and 1435, while R. Vitali ("On Byams pa and Thub chen lha khang of Glo sMos thang", *The Tibet Journal*, XXIV/1, Spring 1999, p. 3) follows another dating and sets the last visit and the completion of the temple in 1448.

2   In 1498 (cf. Vitali, pp. 18–19).

3   However Vitali (p. 21) suggests that the painting of the east wall was carried out either in 1448 or in 1498, giving a slight preference to the former date. Different styles may indeed persist through the centuries, as implied by Vitali himself.

4   The inscriptions found below some deities painted on the south wall, bearing the name of an artist, induced Vitali (p. 20) to suggest that a single master had painted the whole wall. However, from a close scrutiny of the murals, it is clear that it is possible to draw a line dividing them into two different sections, in one of which the loops of the scroll patterns enclosing the many images of Amitabha surrounding the main figures are painted with multicoloured patterns. Furthermore, the styles of the clouds drawn above the two sections differ, one depicting rain-clouds and one with more or less stylized cirrus clouds.

5   In contrast with what is stated by I. Alsop ("The Wall Paintings of Mustang", *Nepal: Old Images, New Insights*, ed. Pratapaditya Pal, Mumbai, 2004, pp. 132 and 135), who describes the ground floor painted only with red, yellow ochre, and black, and the second floor painted in blue, yellow, red, and black.

6   Vitali (p. 7) believes the whole painted programme has been lost.

7   See R. Vitali, *The Kingdoms of Gu.ge Pu.hrang*, Dharamsala, 1996, pp. 532–33.

8   The superior quality of the murals on the west wall makes it hard to believe that the Newar painter Devananda with his assistants also painted the other walls, as stated by Dowman (p. 188).

9   Thanks to Vitali ("On Byams pa and Thub chen lha khang of Glo sMos thang", p. 18), we know that the Maitreya temple was renovated in 1663 and that a new statue with its throne was built, replacing the former image.

CHAPTER 9

The Restoration of Murals
in the Mahamuni Temple of Möntang

Luigi Fieni

The former capital of an ancient kingdom, Lo Möntang hosts unique wall paintings in a 15th-century temple of the Sakya religious order. Accessible only after a three-day horse ride, the Mahamuni (Tupchen) temple was literally falling apart until a team of international specialists arrived to restore it.[1] To assist them in their work, these specialists also trained a number of selected locals as carpenters and restorers.

During this remarkable project, the conservation team grew considerably, from ten to 41 apprentices. A notable precedent was the introduction of women onto the team. Prior to this women had not been allowed to work on any sacred image or site in Lo Möntang; now, however, trained local women greatly outnumber the men.

To develop an optimal restoration plan, the team first completed a thorough study to better understand the manner in which Mahamuni's wall paintings and structures had been executed. It should be emphasized that the majority of wall paintings found in Asia are not fresco paintings; they were executed not on a wet lime-based plaster, but on a dry plaster, and later painted using a non-lime binder. Mahamuni's mural paintings are among the most fascinating examples of 15th-century[2] secco painting in Asia.

The Mahamuni temple consists, at present, of only a vestibule and one vast assembly hall. The hall's rectangular plan, measuring roughly 28 by 22 metres,[3] rises 7.4 metres to the wooden ceiling. The rammed-mud walls are more than 1.6 metres thick at the base. The temple currently counts 35 pillars, though originally there may have been 47.[4] Gigantic images of the Buddha[5] (figure 9.1) and of the Eight Great Bodhisattvas[6] (figure 9.2) dominate Mahamuni's pictorial cycle.

During the restoration, evidence was found of a second storey.[7] According to the Nepalese Institute of Seismology, there were serious earthquakes in the 16th and 18th centuries. These quakes are the probable cause of the first floor's collapse and the destruction of the ground floor's north wall. This scenario would explain the debris accumulated on the northeast side as well as the current position of the temple floor, now well below street level. Excavations carried out in 2000 by Nepal's Department of Archaeology proved that the original street level was 1.6 metres below the present one, and precisely at the same level of the present entrance door to the monastery.[8]

After the earthquake in the 16th or in the 18th century, the north wall was rebuilt as an inward bay, leaving a few square metres of original paintings on this wall, and creating a small chamber in the northeast corner. Though written documentation is lacking, it seems likely the vestibule was added during this repair work. As a result of the damage, the vestibule's original paintings were heavily over-painted thereby rendering dating a difficult task indeed. It has to be said, though, that the stratification of

9.1 Vairochana. Mahamuni temple, east wall above the entrance door, 15th century. Distemper.

the preparatory layers for the murals is the same as in the assembly hall. Moreover, the rammed walls are of the same thickness as the ones forming the assembly hall. Similar to the temple of Maitreya, many separated joints are found in the whole building. This separation could also be attributed to the earthquakes centuries ago.

The wall paintings in the assembly hall can be separated into seven different periods. The earliest paintings from the 15th century are found on the original northern wall, as well as on the eastern, southern, and western walls. The western wall is partly covered by a stupa and by a huge new altar concealing the original paintings. A large part of this wall is heavily painted over, yet several cleaning samples revealed that most of the original paint layer is still present. Unfortunately, the altar's position stymied any restoration work in that area; thus, the original paint layer remains hidden.

The second period (16th or 18th century) consists of a small painted section of the north wall, possibly dating back to the earthquake that destroyed most of this wall. Interestingly, on this section one finds a skilful attempt to restore the damaged painting: rather than paint the section over, the artists matched the new painting to the old one. Moreover, they painted only the surfaces where the paint had been lost. Because these early restorers used a reddish plaster mixture that differed from the original, their interventions are easily identifiable. It should be noted that traditionally restoration is not frequent in the Buddhist world: to make new religious

Opposite
9.2 Mahabodhisattva. Mahamuni temple, east wall, 15th century. Distemper.

9.3 Two bodhisattvas painted by two different artists. Mahamuni temple, south wall, 15th century. Distemper.

images rather than restoring old ones allows the donors to accumulate more merit. Thus, whoever carried out this restoration fully acknowledged the importance and the preciousness of the original murals.

The new north wall was painted during the third period (18th century). Unfortunately, this wall was covered with a rough plaster and cleaning samples revealed only negligible, damaged traces of paint. Structural problems forced us to detach some remains of wall paintings using the stacco technique, removing a thick layer of plaster along with the painted surface. During that operation, several more square metres of earlier paint were revealed from within the new wall; as a result of this discovery, we could not restore the surface murals to their original position. A small museum was built nearby to house the paintings that have been detached.

During a fourth period (19th century), the new north wall was lengthened in the direction of the entrance wall, thereby creating a chamber. A mural was also painted with a long inscription describing the history of the temple. The fifth period (19th century) corresponds to just a fragment on the west section of the new northern wall. A small portion on the upper section of the west wall defines a sixth period (20th century). Finally, a very recent intervention, probably just a few decades old, is evident on the original northern wall, as well as on the southern and western walls. During

9.4 Infrared image showing sketches of mudras, a face and eyes, drawn and pounced – hands are visible on both sides, and a face top left and eyes top right in the mandorla. Mahamuni temple, south wall, 15th century.

9.5 Infrared image showing the main iconometric line on the face. Mahamuni temple, east wall, 15th century.

this last period, a 4-metre-high stone buttress was erected along the murals so as to protect the walls from collapse, and then painted.

Wall paintings are generally never painted directly on the wall surface but on a sequence of overlapping layers; the number of layers varies according to the period of execution and the geographical location. In the specific case of the Mahamuni 15th-century murals, the first layer consisted of a mixture of cow dung, clay, and a considerable amount of vegetal fibre raised to a thickness of 8 millimetres. The second layer is significantly thicker due to the presence of river pebbles mixed with yellowish clay and sand. This mixture creates a very homogeneous coat of 1.3 centimetres which perfectly levels the surface of the walls. On top of this, a final layer of 8 millimetres, composed of very fine greyish clay, creates a particularly smooth surface. The priming layer, consisting of a mixture of white clays and calcite, was not simply applied by brush. Indeed, under raking light no brushstrokes are visible; therefore, the surface must have been polished prior to painting so as to create a mirror-smooth finish. On this surface, artists drew reference lines to arrange all figures symmetrically within each register. From the different styles of painting present, it can be deduced that there were artists from several ateliers working simultaneously. The space was organized in vertical sections each of which included a bodhisattva/Buddha with his attendants. It is clearly visible where each sector begins and ends (figure 9.3).

An infrared camera revealed more details about the execution of the drawings. The presence of dotted traces along the outlines of the figures showed that the technique of pouncing (spolvero) had been used only in the upper sections of the wall paintings (figure 9.4), while in the lower areas just a few lines depict the positions of the body parts to be drawn. Evidence suggests that the masters may have employed their more skilled students in the lower areas and the less skilled in the upper areas (figure 9.5). The diminishing quality of the painting on the wall's upper reaches, combined with the fact that more talented students might not require a stencil to guide them, support this explanation. The masters would have wanted to demonstrate optimal quality in the lower paintings as these are most readily observed. The drawing was followed by the application of relief work (pastiglia) (figure 9.6). A mixture of animal glue and very refined clay was used to emboss the outlines of the jewels and the decorations on the Buddha's robes. Base colours were then applied as needed. All the gilding was executed on a thin coat of realgar so as to warm its final

9.6 Head of bodhisattva. Mahamuni temple, south wall, 15th century. Distemper with pastiglia.

appearance, while the blue was applied on a layer of black or vermilion, so as to reduce the transparency of the pigments. It is worth noting that these same techniques were being employed simultaneously several thousand kilometres away in Europe. While there was a tremendous difference in medium and support[9] of the paint, both cultures were aware of some pigments' transparency and the consequent need for a base colour.

Using a palette that was both rich and unusual, the colours were subsequently applied according to the letters and numbers indicated by the masters. The blue consisted of azurite, lapis lazuli, and indigo, in some cases mixed together so as to obtain different hues (figure 9.7). For the red and orange, hematite and vermilion were used alternately or mixed together. The green consisted of the typical malachite pigments, while the brown was a mixture of malachite, azurite, and vermilion (figure 9.8). To give the appearance of shading to the figures and to their Chinese-style brocade

9.7 Detail showing kirtimukha. Mahamuni temple, south wall, 15th century. Distemper.

9.8 Atlas figure. Mahamuni temple, west wall, 15th century. Distemper.

draperies and garments, lacquer was applied. The gold was used either in gold leaf or powder form to create aesthetically elegant results (figure 9.9). The gilded pastiglia is particularly striking when the gold creates natural shadows in the sunlight. A thick varnish coating made from tree secretions finished the work. It is this final layer that has caused problems in the restoration of the underlying paint layer.

Before any work could take place on the wall paintings and statues, the temple's abbot had to perform an important ceremony. This ceremony, known as arga, used a mirror-like metal disc to collect all the divinities' spirits present in the temple's images. Once all the spirits represented in the wall paintings and statues were collected, the ritual mirror was wrapped in a

9.9 Detail of mahabodhisattva in figure 9.2. Mahamuni temple, east wall, 15th century. Distemper.

sacred scarf so that the spirits could not escape. The swathed mirror was then hung on a temple pillar that no one was allowed to touch. In this way, local religious adherents believed that the divinities could avoid harm from the chemicals and syringes used during the restoration work.

The enormity of our task became clear the very first time we stepped into the building. The original varnish was completely darkened by centuries of ageing, and smoke deposits from butter lamps had turned many areas of the paintings entirely black. Over a period of six centuries, earthquakes had caused several cracks and a random separation from the walls of the preparatory layers of the wall paintings. In many cases this separation had provoked the collapse of the pictorial layer. Rising dampness to a height of more than three metres around the temple base had destroyed the lower sections of the wall paintings. An unusual flaking of the paint layer had produced an unsystematic and widespread loss of paintings here, as in the Maitreya temple.

Such damage had turned these decaying temples into forgotten places, no longer used by the local community. On occasion, a few butter lamps would be lit, but monks refused to perform any rituals because a damaged or defiled image cannot be the object of worship.

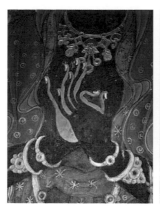

9.10 Detail of bodhisattva showing the cleaning process. Mahamuni temple, east wall, 15th century. Distemper.

The conservation team's first task was to train a group of local farmers as skilled restorers. Through description, demonstration, and practice, the apprentices gradually became adept in all the necessary restorative techniques. Their actual practice began on the more recent paintings in Mahamuni, so that they could develop their abilities and skills prior to working on the 15th-century paintings.

Four working seasons were required to fix the flaking paint layer and to stabilize the detached preparatory layers. First, particulates were removed from the flakes of painting; each flake was then unrolled back into position using specific spatulas and organic binders purposely studied and tested for restoration. Later, the spaces between preparatory layers were filled with a gluing solution made from the same clays used in the original technique.

Given that different pigments react differently to the same solvent, a variety of chemicals were employed to clean Mahamuni's many colours. Azurite, lapis lazuli, and malachite were cleaned with a basic solution (figure 9.10), while organic chemicals were employed to remove the varnish from the other colours. To clean the gilding, a special cotton compress, soaked in organic solvents, was applied to the exceedingly resistant varnish.

Our work involved not only the temple's paintings but its very structure as well. Deep cracks traversing the wall's thickness were present in all corners. In addition, a painted stone buttress had been constructed around the temple's perimeter to reinforce walls weakened by rising damp. Indeed, a good portion of the northern, eastern, and southern walls had already eroded to a height of four metres.

To restore beauty and strength to the temple, cracks were cleaned by removing the straw, dung, mud, stones, and bones that villagers had used to fill them. Later, these cracks were plastered under the level of paint, and a grouting mixture composed of gluing solution and local clays was injected to fill the gap. The stone buttress, bulging more than 30 centimetres from the wall, was removed section by section to prevent any risk of collapse. A new wall was slowly built in its place and subsequently plastered under the level of paint with a mixture of clays and straw that imitated the original composition (figure 9.11).

In spite of all the difficulties during the restoration process, it was breathtaking to see the bright original colours slowly coming back to life. I remember well the reaction of the Raja of Mustang when, in 1999, he came to observe our first cleaning sample. He congratulated us on our painting skills. When we told him that we had not painted anything but simply removed the dirt from the original paintings, the king was utterly astounded.

Perhaps even more satisfying, I have witnessed the temple's rebirth. With the passing of the years, local people have begun to return to the temple more and more frequently. After so many centuries of neglect, it was moving to see a coloured powder mandala being slowly and carefully created by patient monks in one of the many rituals performed since the Mahamuni's renewal (figure 9.12). While the conservation team's achievements were a source of great satisfaction, what was even more delightful was that the community could finally see their temple and deities reborn.

9.11 Ratnasambhava painting with the underlying wall being replaced. Mahamuni temple, south wall, 15th century. Distemper.

9.12 A ritual being performed in the Mahamuni temple assembly hall, August 30, 2004.

FIGURE ACKNOWLEDGEMENTS
All photographs by Luigi Fieni.

NOTES

1   The project started in 1999 and was completed in 2004. It was funded by the American Himalayan Foundation and the restoration was undertaken in collaboration with John Sanday Associates and with the help of an Italian team of conservators.

2   Thanks to R. Vitali ("On Byams pa and Thub chen lha khang of Glo sMos thang", *The Tibet Journal*, XXIV/1, Spring 1999, p. 4), we have records of a religious ceremony being held in the temple in 1472. I. Alsop ("The Wall Paintings of Mustang", *Nepal: Old Images, New Insights*, ed. Pratapaditya Pal, Mumbai, 2004, p. 136) sets the consecration of the building in 1471. Although the monastery could have been finished earlier or, perhaps, was still under construction, we have a period in which to collocate the construction work.

3   Alsop (p. 136) reports 28 by 18 metres.

4   Vitali (p. 11) reports 49 pillars because he includes two pillars supporting a roofed skylight. In my opinion, the skylight was an opening to an upper storey that does not exist any longer: the skylight was a later addition. The two pillars were set up in the vestibule, which at present contains pillars and capitals taken from the nearby temple of Maitreya.

5   Seven in the south wall and possibly the same number in the destroyed north wall. Vairochana occupies the centre of the east wall, facing the main statue, and two images of Shakyamuni, one of which is covered by a coating of plaster and hidden by the statues on the main altar, are found on the west wall.

6   There are six in the east wall and one in both south and east walls. The attributes identifying each deity are depicted in the flowers they hold.

7   Vitali (p. 11) believes that the temple was one-storeyed.

8   This implies that Vitali (p. 13) is wrong when suggesting that the floor of the temple was lowered on purpose.

9   Lime in Europe was mostly used as both medium and support (fresco technique) while in geo-cultural Tibet animal glue was frequently used as medium and clay as support for the wall paintings (one of the several secco techniques).

CHAPTER 10

Bönpo and Buddhist Art in 20th-century Lo

Chiara Bellini

The aim of traditional sacred art is to aid the believer or the worshipper in meditation and in the performance of rituals. The intrinsic value of a work of art – according to the criteria by which it is judged in Indo-Tibetan cultures – lies primarily in its function and not in its aesthetic qualities, let alone its antiquity.[1] Accordingly, the religious art of Lo has played an active role in the community to this very day and is appreciated regardless of age by those for whom it is created. The very notion of "ancient", a Western concept, assumes different connotations from the Indo-Tibetan point of view, suggesting something out of date or simply old.

In this cultural context, while the restorations funded by foreign foundations have increased local awareness of the historical value of ancient art, it would be untrue to say that Indo-Tibetan aesthetic values have been altered or redefined. On the contrary, they remain anchored to the overriding importance ascribed to the image's function in relation to spiritual practice. Therefore, in order to understand Indo-Tibetan art, we have to cast aside our cultural preconceptions and rely on the parameters of those who commission, make, and use religious images.

Examples of contemporary painting and sculpture in Lo can be seen in certain Buddhist and Bönpo stupas, temples, and monasteries. Bön, a heterodox form of Buddhism,[2] is still practised in certain villages despite its gradual decline in Lo. Contemporary Bön wall paintings and sculptures can be found in the two main religious structures in the village of Lubrak, two hours' walk from Jomsom: the temple of Püntsokling and the monastery of Gönpuk, about half an hour's walk from the temple.

The temple of Püntsokling was founded in the 19th century by Karu Drupwang Tendzin Rinchen who was born in Western Tibet in 1801.[3] Inside it there is a group of nine painted clay sculptures, which are presumably contemporary or made in the late 19th century. These statues are interesting examples of popular clay sculpture. Around 1.5 metres high, they are arranged along the main, far wall of the temple and on the right-hand wall, as one enters. The first statue portrays Tönpa Sherap Miwo, the founder of Bön. Originally from Tazik and active in Zhangzhung,[4] he is regarded as having achieved enlightenment and takes the place of the historical Buddha Shakyamuni in the Bön tradition. From the iconographic point of view, Sherap Miwo is depicted as Shakyamuni, with a monk's habit, hair done up in a bun, legs folded in the lotus position, and arms in the gesture of calling the earth to witness his enlightenment.

Next to Tönpa Sherap stands the statue of Nampar Gyelwa, the emanation of Sherap as the invincible subduer of demons and eliminator of obstacles[5] (figure 10.1). He is portrayed with his right arm raised, the palm turned slightly outwards, in the gesture of warding off demons. His left arm instead rests on his knee, in the mudra of repose, while his face

10.1 Nampar Gyelwa, Püntsokling temple, Lubrak. Painted clay.

is set in a ferocious grimace. This sculpture has a considerable mandorla, decorated with lions with brahmins in their jaws, dragons eating baby nagas, creatures that are half-human and half-snake, writhing sea monsters (makaras) and a Garuda at the top. These details are not mere decorations, as the description of this particular type of mandorla in chapter five of the 12-volume biography of Tönpa Sherap, devoted to Nampar Gyelwa, makes clear.

Next to the statue of Nampar Gyelwa is a beautiful white clay figure of Künzang Gyelwa Düpa, seated in the meditation posture (figure 10.2). Künzang Gyelwa Düpa has five faces bearing peaceful expressions, and ten arms, the first two of which are held at chest height in the gesture of equanimity. The palms of the hands are turned towards the observer and are decorated with the symbols of the sun and the moon, inscribed with the syllables "A" and "MA", symbolizing method and wisdom.[6] The divinity holds a victory banner, a swastika, and the wheel of the law in three of

10.2 Künzang Gyelwa Düpa, Püntsokling temple, Lubrak. Painted clay.

10.3 Drenpa Namkha, Püntsokling temple, Lubrak. Painted clay.

his right hands, while the corresponding left three grasp a bow and arrow, a lasso, and a hook. Two other hands rest on his knees in the gesture of repose.

A third sculpture represents the tantric manifestation of the master Drenpa Namkha regarded as a form of divinity, in sexual union with his mate, the dakini Öden Barma (figure 10.3). This figure is well known both in the Bön as well as in the Buddhist Nyingmapa and Kagyüpa traditions as the symbol of a non-sectarian religious outlook. Next to Drenpa Namkha is a portrait of Nyammé Sherap Gyeltsen (1356–1415), from Eastern Tibet, who was responsible for structuring the Bönpo monastic order and was the founder in 1405 of the monastery of Menri, in Central Tibet.[7] This monastery was a leading light in the spiritual, monastic, and liturgical life of the Bönpo religion until the Cultural Revolution forced its thirty-second abbot to flee to India. The monastery was completely demolished and later rebuilt in 1984. By then, a new Menri monastery had been erected in 1969 in Dolanji, Himachal Pradesh, India, reacquiring its ancient status as a model for all Bönpo communities under its thirty-third abbot.

On the right-hand wall can be seen the image of Lubrakpa, identifiable from the inscription painted on the lotus petal throne on which the figure is seated in meditation. Lubrakpa is the epithet used to refer to Trashi Gyeltsen, a Bönpo master who lived in the 13th century and to whom the above-mentioned monastery of Gönpuk is dedicated.[8] The story of Trashi Gyeltsen, also known as the "Protector of Living Beings" is painted on the east wall of the temple. According to tradition, Lubrakpa withdrew into the cave to meditate for nine years, nine months, and nine days and this temple was subsequently built over the site. After repeated restoration and a final collapse, the temple was re-erected in modern times thanks to funding from the Danish Embassy in Kathmandu. In 2002 the temple was decorated with a cycle of paintings by the Nepalese artist Aku Gochen, from the Helambu area of Nepal, who lives in Bodhnath, east of Kathmandu.

The Gönpuk cycle of paintings depicts certain divinities in the Bönpo pantheon together with the painted narrative of the temple founder's life. Of particular interest in the first group of figures, depicted on the southern wall, is the representation of the red Apsé Dungmar, holding a victory banner in one hand and an owl in the other (figure 10.4). In this case, Apsé's hair, normally hidden by a helmet, is shown blown about by the swirling wind that spirals round the flames surrounding the figure. Sipè Gyelmo, the last figure on the wall, with her multiple limbs and attributes, is the Bönpo equivalent of Penden Lhamo, the Buddhist protectress of Tibet, whose iconography originates from that of the Hindu goddess Durga.

On the west wall are depicted four other figures. One of them, Jamma ("Loving Kindness"), is a female divinity coloured yellow, whose name is the feminine equivalent of Jampa, the Tibetan name for the Buddhist bodhisattva Maitreya. However, iconographically, this divinity has no connection with Maitreya, being much more closely related to the Buddhist divinity Tara. She is depicted with a third, vertical eye between her eyebrows

10.4 Apsé Dungmar, Gönpuk monastery, Lubrak. Distemper.

exactly like Tara and, like her, she is shown in her eight-fold form as the protectress against eight dangers. Here again, the Indian model for much Bönpo iconography is obvious. A large proportion of Bönpo doctrine, which, as David Snellgrove has argued, represents a heterodox form of Buddhism, is also certainly Indian in origin. Bönpo rituals, religious beliefs, and iconography are largely similar to those of Buddhism and they also have their roots in the Indian tradition.

The figure of Jamma is followed by three masters raised to the level of divinities, the most important one being Drenpa Namkha, who according to tradition was instrumental in the spread of Bön during the 8th century.

The north wall is partly covered by a stone altar and by the entrance to the cave where Trashi Gyeltsen meditated, and partly by three painted divinities: Tapiritsa, Künzang Gyelwa Düpa, and Zhangzhung Meri.

Tapiritsa is one of the most esoteric figures in the Bön pantheon and perhaps one of the most frequently represented. This master is portrayed shorn of clothing, jewellery, and attributes, sitting in the lotus position and making the gesture of meditation, surrounded by a round mandorla of rainbow rays. The rainbow also occurs as a symbol in Buddhism, but is more commonly found in Bön. Tapiritsa's chief characteristic is his human appearance, and as a result he is coloured pink and has no additional arms or legs. The straightforwardness typical of Tapiritsa is matched by the key concepts of the esoteric Dzokchen[9] doctrine, of which the founder of the temple was a practitioner. Dzokchen regards the human condition as "perfect", a state in which nothing needs to be changed. At the heart of this doctrine lies the notion that every moment in life is to be lived trying to maintain one's natural state, *rikpa*, namely "knowledge", which is often obscured by ignorance or deflected by karmic influences. Under the image of Tapiritsa is painted the Tibetan letter "A" enclosed within

Opposite
10.5 Künzang Gyelwa Düpa and Zhangzhung Meri, Gönpuk monastery, Lubrak. Distemper.

10.6 Zhangzhung Meri, detail of figure 10.5, Gönpuk monastery, Lubrak. Distemper.

a multicoloured spherical drop, *tikle*, which in the Dzokchen tradition represents the primordial, pure human condition beyond dualistic concepts. Tapiritsa's hagiographies claim he achieved the so-called "rainbow body", the dissolution of the body into light of five different colours, corresponding to the five elements.

One aspect of Bön iconography, also ascribable to Indian origins, is the use of sacred syllables as the attributes of the various divinities. This applies not only to Tapiritsa, but also to Künzang Gyelwa Düpa (figure 10.5), who bears the syllables "A" and "MA" inscribed on the palms of his main hands, as was seen in his depiction in the previous temple. Next to Künzang Gyelwa Düpa is Meri, a ferocious divinity who embodies the "Fire Mountain of Shangshung" (figures 10.5 and 10.6). His image is shown in a dynamic posture, with all 18 arms and six legs in motion, and his precisely depicted hair blowing in the wind. A large mandorla of flames surrounds the image, lending the already terrifying, three-headed figure surmounted by six animal heads an even more ferocious mien.

In the middle of the temple's east wall is a large painting depicting the biography of Lubrakpa, namely Trashi Gyeltsen (figure 10.7). His life and deeds[10] are crucially important in the history and spread of Bön in Lo. The cycle of paintings illustrates his human and spiritual biography. The scenes are accompanied by captions describing the images drawn.

The cycle opens with the representation of Trashi Gyeltsen's father, the "great" Yantön Sherap Gyeltsen (1077–1141?), who was from southwest Tibet. He was a member of the Yangal clan and travelled to Lo to seek the Bön master, Ronggom Tokmé Zhikpo, who lived in western Lo, from whom he learned the teachings of the "Dzokchen Oral Tradition of Shangshung",[11] becoming one of its chief promulgators. The following images illustrate the life of the young Trashi Gyeltsen, first with his wife, then with his three children. It was only after the death of his beloved consort that Trashi Gyeltsen devoted himself totally to Bönpo, and he is portrayed as he receives instruction from the master Shentön Yeshé Lotrö.[12]

The scenes concerned with the famous conversion of a demon, Kyerang Drakmé ("Self-Generated Without Fear"), living in the mountains of Lubrak, are among the most beautiful and most curious of the narrative. The demon performs a series of evil actions against the Bönpo master, but is converted in the end, becoming a protector of the doctrine himself. The cycle also includes a depiction of the cave where "the master Trashi Gyeltsen performs the 'Mountain of Fire' ritual", as can be read in the inscription.[13] In memory of this time spent in isolation, the lama left his footprint in a rock that is still visible today at the entrance to the cave.

The final scene in the cycle depicts Trashi Gyeltsen's spiritual fulfilment (see figure 1.5), the moment when his body is transformed into a rainbow.[14]

10.7 Episodes from Trashi Gyeltsen's life, Gönpuk monastery, Lubrak. Distemper.

10.8 Lubrak Sungma Sinpo Kyerang, Gönpuk monastery, Lubrak. Distemper.

Following the iconographic programme of the temple in the anti-clockwise direction, at the very end can be found the unusual image of Lubrak Sungma Sinpo Kyerang (figure 10.8). This is a local divinity, representing Kyerang Drakmé, the demon converted by Trashi Gyeltsen and turned into a protector of the doctrine, a notion incorporated in his very name, which means "at once the demon and protector of Lubrak". This figure has two fierce faces, the main one wearing a helmet, the other having the same features as the face of Kyerang Drakmé depicted in the cycle portraying the life of Trashi Gyeltsen. Here, however, a boar's head protruding from the demon's hair is added.

One example of contemporary traditional Buddhist art is the cycle of paintings in the Sakyapa temple in Geling, south of Möntang. These paintings were made by Tulachan Shashi Dhoje, whose name appears in a long inscription in the entrance porch. Another name in the same inscription, Chögyel Tendzin, is perhaps the artist's second name or one

Opposite
10.9 Gurgön, Geling temple. Distemper.

of his assistants'. The work was begun on May 18, 1991 and completed on October 2 the following year.

On the southeastern part of the wall, in which is set the entrance to the assembly hall, are gathered a number of protectors of the doctrine: Gurgön (figure 10.9), Penden Lhamo (figure 10.10), the four-headed Gönpo, and two other versions of Gurgön and Penden Lhamo. The last figure painted on the southwestern section of the wall is Künga Zangpo (1382–1456) whose importance for the renaissance of the faith in Lo has been discussed elsewhere in this book (see chapter 1).

The daylight filters into the assembly hall through a lantern set in the middle of the ceiling. The interior walls are painted, the southern section being decorated with pictures of the historical Buddha with his favourite disciples, the 16 sthavira, with their two attendants. The eastern side is decorated with a large picture of the Indian master Nagarjuna accompanied by a water sprite shown as she emerges daintily from the waves to proffer a text to the master. The artist's name (Tulachan Shashi Dhoje) can be made out next to the figure. The northern side depicts the great master Künga Nyingpo together with other masters from the Sakya lineage.

10.10 Penden Lhamo, Geling temple. Distemper.

A further example of contemporary Buddhist art in the kingdom of Lo is Tupten Sampel Ling, the Sakyapa monastery of Kagbeni (Kak). It was founded in 1429 by the master Tenpè Gyeltsen and contains a cycle of wall paintings commissioned by the present abbot of the monastery and executed towards the late 1970s by a Tamang artist living in Bodhnath. These paintings are not as fine as those described above, but are nonetheless of a certain interest from an iconographic and compositional point of view, as they reflect their patron's taste and reveal the monastery's financial circumstances. Lo used to be an economically and spiritually thriving kingdom, as demonstrated by the ancient paintings in the Lo Möntang temples, which were built and decorated using rare and precious materials, such as lapis lazuli and gold. By contrast, the finances of contemporary patrons have often proved unequal to the expense, and extra funds, even from abroad, have had to be sought to commission restorations or new artworks, as in the case of the Bönpo temple of Lubrak.

On the east wall, where the entrance to the temple is situated, stand the four guardian kings divided into pairs, along with Avalokiteshvara and a beautiful image of a White Tara (figure 10.11). Next to her, at the northern end of the wall, can be seen the representation of the "Parable of

10.11 White Tara and the "Parable of Collaboration", Tupten Sampel Ling, Kagbeni. Distemper.

Collaboration", an ancient "edifying tale" in which an elephant, a monkey, a hare, and a bird join forces and use their separate skills to pick a fruit, eat it, scatter its seeds over the ground, and nurture them (figure 10.11).

The glass cases along the west wall house an important collection of metal sculptures from different periods arranged on shelves around two large images of Sakya masters (figure 10.12). Near the 81-centimetre-high sculpture of one of them is a copper image of Tara (see figure 10.12, lower right) cast by the lost-wax technique – its delicate facial features and sinuous lines making it a fine example of contemporary Newar sculpture. Newar sculptors from the Nepal Valley have always worked in Tibetan and Himalayan monasteries. New clients continue even today to follow the age-old tradition and commission their sculpture from these skilful artists. The complex techniques of modelling, casting, and carving have been handed down intact from father to son and from master to pupil over the centuries. The great contemporary Newar artists strictly follow the techniques inherited from their masters and keep to traditional iconographic and iconometric models. Some

10.12 Sakya master, Tupten Sampel Ling, Kagbeni. 81 cm.

perform their work as an integral part of their spiritual exercises, a sort of creative meditation requiring concentration and an awareness of one's every gesture.

In spite of the shortage of financial resources, the Lo monasteries continue to press ahead with their restoration, commissioning paintings and clay and metal sculptures from local craftsmen or artists of neighbouring areas. Private chapels also contain series of contemporary paintings and sculptures. So, although the inhabitants of Lo have certainly had to face economic hardship and have perhaps experienced a reduction in spiritual vitality and in the awareness of their artistic and cultural heritage, they have certainly not lost their will to preserve and pass on their tradition as well as their social and religious values.

FIGURE ACKNOWLEDGEMENTS
All photographs by Chiara Bellini.

NOTES
1   E. Lo Bue, "Tibetan Aesthetics versus Western Aesthetics in the Appreciation of Religious Art", *Images of Tibet in the 19th and 20th Centuries*, ed. M. Esposito, Paris, 2008, pp. 687–704.

2   D. Snellgrove, *Nine Ways of Bon*, Oxford, 1967.

3   C. Ramble and M. Kind, "Bonpo monasteries and temples of the Himalayan region", *A Survey of Bonpo Monasteries and Temples in Tibet and the Himalaya*, ed. S.G. Karmay and Y. Nagano, Delhi, 2008, p. 671.

4   Because of insufficient historical information, it is relatively difficult to locate these regions exactly. Zhangzhung included Western Tibet and some regions surrounding it. It was conquered by the Tibetan emperor Songtsen Gampo during the first half of the 7th century. Tazik is "vaguely identifiable with Persia" (D. Snellgrove and H. Richardson, *A Cultural History of Tibet*, Boston/London, 1995, p. 99).

5   P. Kvaerne, *The Bon Religion of Tibet*, London, 2001, p. 33.

6   S.G. Karmay and J. Watt, *Bon, The Magic Word: The Indigenous Religion of Tibet*, New York/London, 2007, p. 48.

7   S.G. Karmay and Y. Nagano, *New Horizons in Bon Studies*, Delhi, 2004, p. 313.

8   Ramble and Kind, "Bonpo monasteries and temples of the Himalayan region", pp. 671–76.

9   G. Baroetto, *Il libro tibetano dei sei lum: L'insegnamento zogcen di Tapi Hritsa*, Roma, 2002, pp. 7–10.

10   L. Chandra and T. Namdak, *History and Doctrine of Bon po Nispanna Yoga*, New Delhi, 1968. See also T. Namdak, *Sources for a History of Bon: A collection of rare manuscripts from Bsam-gling Monastery in Dolpo (Northwestern Nepal)*, Dolanji, 1972.

11   *rDzogs chen Zhang zhung snyan rgyud.*

12   *Gshen chen ye shes blo gros kyi drung du so so thar pa'i sdom pa mnos.*

13   *Yang ston pa kshis rgyal mtshan sgom phu(g) tu me ri'i bsgrubs pa mdzad.*

14   *Dzogs pa chen po zhang zhung ston rgyud la grub thob pa yang ston bla ma bKra shis rgyal mtshan ni dgung lo brgyad u tsa nga la dgongs pa bon dbyings su 'ja' lus 'od skur sngas rgyas so.*

CHAPTER 11

Reviving a Sacred Place:
The Hermitage of Samdrupling

Maie Kitamura

The Lopas (people of Lo) have defied the region's physical constraints of high altitude and extreme climate and built settlements, practised agriculture and breeding, and perpetuated their religious traditions here for centuries. Thus, all along the Kali Gandaki river, right from its source, many sacred spots, and places of worship, caves or constructions, have come into existence, the choice of their location being also determined by the presence of symbolical elements in the landscape.

Lo Möntang was built in the 15th century when the first king of Lo decided to found a city and to settle in it with his people, and has served since then as the region's economic and religious centre. It has reached us almost intact more than six centuries later.

Well before the foundation of Lo Möntang there were places of retreat such as Samdrupling ("Island of the Fulfilment of Aspirations"). The oral tradition is hardly precise regarding the age of its foundation, and written evidence is scanty. Nevertheless, it may be suggested that the establishment of Samdrupling hermitage is related to the existence of Lo Gekar, the oldest Buddhist centre in Lo whose foundation goes back to the 8th century and is linked to Guru Padmasambhava.

Over the centuries Samdrupling went through a period of decline. Today, with the revival of interest in Lo Möntang's buildings, the local clergy is planning to restore the site to its former role and importance. Because of the hermitage's present state of ruin, this project has to combine structural conservation with the restoration of decorative elements, as has been done at the better conserved monuments of the capital, following the cultural revival in Lo.

HISTORY OF THE SITE

The high valley of the Kali Gandaki provides a route across the Himalaya that human beings have taken advantage of through the millennia. For our knowledge of the most ancient part of this region's history from Tibetan sources we are indebted to Tibetologists such as Giuseppe Tucci, David Jackson, and Roberto Vitali (see the list of references in chapter 1).

When I was in Lo during May 2005 the history of Samdrupling was related to me by Lama Pasang, head monk of the Tsechen-Shedrupling monastic school in the Chödé monastery. According to tradition, the monastery and hermitage of Samdrupling were established in the 12th century by Lama Ronggom, disciple of Künga Nyingpo (1092–1158), one of the five founders of the Sakya religious order. Lama Ronggom would have stayed at Samdrupling for several years. The founding of the monastery is probably linked to the presence of an ancient meditation cave, located opposite the temple, on the right bank of the Kali Gandaki, to the south. Called Samdrupling cave, its external facade is painted in white and encircled by a

11.1 View of the Samdrupling ridge overlooking the valley to the west. Photograph: Luigi Fieni, 2006.

red painted frame, a sign of its sacred nature. Traces of mural paintings can be found inside the cave, which also contained religious manuscripts, painted scrolls, and statues, at present conserved in the Chödé monastery. The cave still served as a hermitage for nuns until some 20 years ago, but is now abandoned.

In the course of time, Samdrupling became a centre of religious practices of the Sakya order and in 1527 Lowo Khenchen Sönam Lhündrup (1456–1532), a religious figure renowned as far as Tibet, completed an important work of his there.[1]

In the historical narrative, the *Tsarang Molla*, it is said that around 1780 King Wangyel Dorjé, who received the teachings of great Nyingmapa and Sakyapa masters, established a monastic centre in Samdrupling, endowing it with enough wealth to make regular offerings.[2]

Under the reign of Jampel Dradül during the first half of the 19th century, the monastery of Drakar Tekchenling was integrated with the Chödé of Lo Möntang. The lamas of Samdrupling also settled down in Chödé and the monastery of Samdrupling then became a nunnery. Jampel Dradül invited religious personalities from Tibet, but his spiritual master remained the Lama Chökyi Nyima from the monastery of Samdrupling.[3] The nunnery must have retained a certain importance within Lo's religious and cultural life at the time.

Lama Chökyi Nyima, as the head of the Chödé in Lo Möntang, created a convent in the Chödé monastery, to which he transferred the nuns of Samdrupling. Samdrupling then became a monastery of the Drukpa Kagyü tradition. The presence of a *tülku*, or incarnate lama, may have contributed to Samdrupling retaining its role as monastery during the first half of the 20th century. The present derelict state of the monastery seems to be related to this lama's death in 1947; Samdrupling was then looted of its statues and ritual objects, and what could be saved is presently conserved in the Chödé at Lo Möntang.

Then Samdrupling apparently became a sky burial place. During the second half of the 20th century, the temple's wooden structures were unrigged and reused in the construction of new buildings in Lo Möntang.[4] Since 2004, the Mustang District Administration has offered resources for the restoration of the temple, where monks of the Chödé wish to re-establish a retreat centre in their Sakyapa tradition.

THE SITE

Samdrupling is located about 5 kilometres west of Lo Möntang, at an altitude of over 4,150 metres on the west edge of the Thakkhola Fault. There stand the ruins of a small temple, close to the escarpment limiting the ridge on the west, precisely on an ancient terrace located at mid-height on the left bank of a seasonal dry river (figure 11.1).

The site presents the character of a scree resulting from the erosion of the rock face, the deposits accumulating at the foot of reliefs, forming a "fan" or accumulation zone. This indicates that we are on the fault's edge.[5] Such soil composition underlines the precarious nature of the monastery's situation, which may have contributed to its abandonment. However, the site of Samdrupling meets the ideal geomantic conditions for the implantation of sacred architecture: a mountain in the background, representing the pure domain of gods, a pathway to the east, a large expanse to the west, and a river with its vegetation to the south. While the place offered physical protection, its sacred geography suggests that, as is always the case in Buddhist architecture, the site was not chosen at random. The limits of the valley are symbolically marked by numerous cairns (*lhatho*) and stupas.

The valley of Samdrupling, bordered to the east by high mountains, stretches out downstream from west to east towards the city of Lo Möntang. The temple abuts the hillside to the north, facing the seasonal river in the valley bed to the south. The vegetation of the valley is of steppe character with thorny bushes, of *Caragana pygmaea* and *Lonicera spinosa* types, which grow at over 4,000 m. Legend tells us that Samdrupling Valley used to be wooded with juniper; only one is left today, a hundred-year-old tree standing on the north-south axis of the temple, a sacred element as expressed by its red painted trunk. This tree by the river is the temporary camping place of nomadic people who settle there during the high season. A paddock for livestock, built of river stones, suggests that this place is regularly occupied.

THE RUINS

The traces of the built site extend over an area of approximately 3,000 square metres (figure 11.2). Numerous foundations and wall bases of flat stones can be observed. A small temple is erected at the centre of the ruins (figure 11.3). It is composed of a square-plan cella, of circa 30 spans (6.6 metres) per side, preceded by a small courtyard flanked by two rooms (a chapel to the west

11.2 Sketch plan of the existing built site, Samdrupling, 2005.

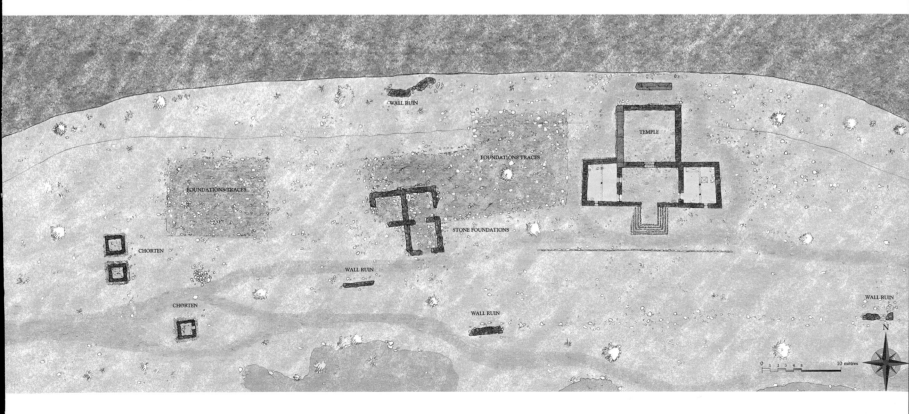

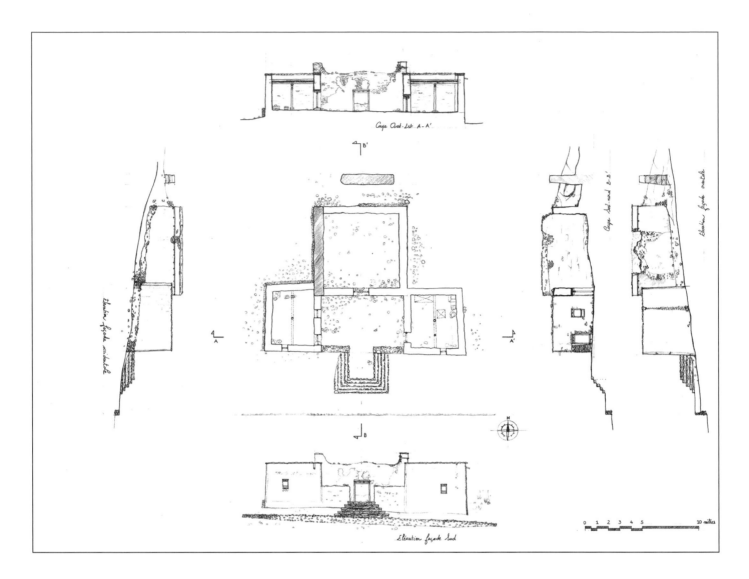

Caps Quel-Est A-A'

Caps lest-ard B-B'

Élévation façade Sud

and a kitchen to the east). The entrance from the south comes up a flight of five stairs into the courtyard (figure 11.4). This layout corresponds to the evolution of an ancient Tibetan plan (11th–13th centuries) itself derived from early temples in Central Asia.[6]

It is interesting to note the composite assembly of materials. The walls are mainly built in flat stone masonry roughcast with earth and coated with a layer of fine earth made of limestone. The coating is left in the natural earth colour with traces of red paint at some places (figure 11.5). Two walls stand apart from the rest: the west wall of the cella, built in the traditional rammed-earth style (*gyang*), and a piece of wall situated outside, behind the temple, parallel to the northern wall of the cella. The coating of this part of the wall is made out of an extremely fine earth and bears traces of paintings.

The *gyang* walls are more ancient than the rest of the temple. It seems that the present building is the result of a late restoration, and we can suppose that the original temple was entirely built in *gyang*. Additions to and demolitions of temple structures being a constant characteristic of all Buddhist monasteries, not only in the Western Himalaya, it is extremely difficult to date the different parts, the difficulty being increased by the timeless character of earth material.

11.3 Sketch plan of the temple ruins, Samdrupling, 2005.

Opposite
11.4 Main facade of the Samdrupling temple with the courtyard preceding the cella flanked by two secondary rooms. Photograph: Luigi Fieni, 2006.
11.5 View of the Samdrupling temple from the west. Photograph: Luigi Fieni, 2006.

The other ruins form a geometric pattern of assembled quadrangular elements in plan. The implantation of ancient constructions follows a double direction: one strictly oriented towards the temple, following the north-south and east-west directions, and another following an oblique axis along the curve of the valley towards the cave.

Stupas are objects of veneration symbolizing the Mind of the Buddha. They also serve as spatial markers and define habitable as well as sacred areas. On the road from Lo Möntang to Samdrupling, numerous groups of stupas punctuate the way. An important group of 15 stupas precedes the ridge pass that overlooks the valley. This group, called Chaksa Gang, was erected to protect the villages from flooding.[7] Another group provided with two rough sandstone mani walls (of stone tablets with the inscription "*om mani padme hum*") marks the direction of access to the temple (figure 11.6).

Other stupas mark symbolic points in the landscape: facing the temple, on the right bank, two such structures overlook a cave which might have been used for meditation. To the west of the temple stand three stupas, each measuring over 3 metres per side. A smaller stupa topped by a Buddhist flagpole stands nearby.

11.6 Groups of chortens and mani walls marking the direction of the access to the temple. Photograph: Luigi Fieni, 2006.

THE HERMITAGE REANIMATION PROJECT

In 2005, the monks of Chödé expressed the wish to restore the temple and to create a meditation centre for themselves and for the Lopa community at large. This desire led to an architectural project, raising the issue of the destiny of sacred places and their survival. The project was commissioned by Lama Pasang during my stay at Lo Mönthang in May 2005, when I was conducting field research relating to the wall of the city.

Reviving a sacred place involves taking into consideration the constraints of customs and traditions, and requires adjustment with practices and ways of life that have been perpetuated and yet have evolved through time. Reinvesting a space with the sacred element means going beyond simple restitution, not limited to the objects, but considering the practices and their evolution, as well as the physical, symbolic, and social environments.

The conceptualization of the project has required a constant dialogue between the monks, who express their desires and those of their community, and the architect, whose proposals are influenced by his/her own vision. This dialogue has nourished the project's development, so as to succeed in elaborating a habitable whole that is of practical use besides preserving ancient traditions and practices and giving life to terms such as conservation, restoration, heritage….

The lamas of Chödé have probably been influenced by the evolution of religious activities of various orders, hailing from the Kathmandu Valley since 1959, from India, and from the Western world. The project consists of two distinct interventions: the rehabilitation of the temple and the creation of a meditation centre. The interventions on the temple would respect its initial dimensions and consist of recreating the space suggested by the surviving traces. The centre would welcome religious people, but also secular people, be they Lopas, pilgrims from elsewhere, or even strangers to the

11.7 Project: main level plan.

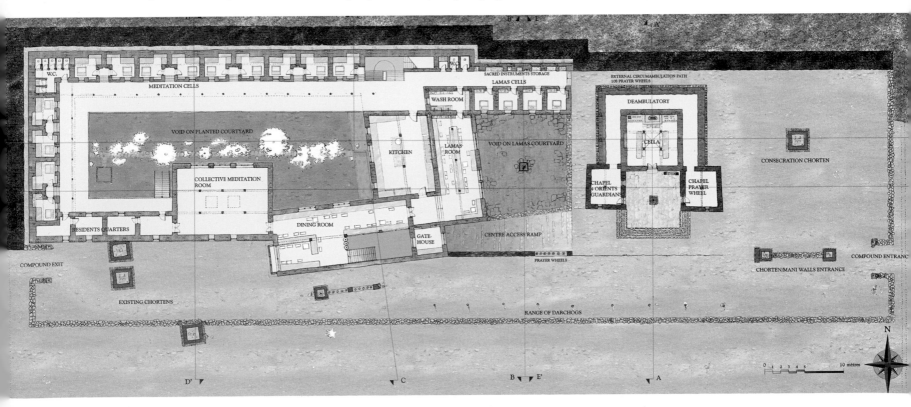

11.8 Project: overview from southwest to northeast.

11.9 Project: A-A' section through the temple cella.

11.10 Project: C-C' section through the entrance courtyard, dining room, planted courtyard, and meditation cells.

11.11 Project: west-east section through the temple cella and deambulatory (detail of X-X' section).

Tibetan cultural world and its religion. The centre would be articulated around a double spatial system: one part would be reserved for the monks while the other one would be open to all (figure 11.7).

The project tries to articulate existing elements to form a coherent system at a landscape scale (figure 11.8). Water, trees, stupas, ruins, cave, are the tangible signs of a system that defines all at once a sacred area as well as a natural and a built landscape. The generated layout superimposes itself on the existing layout, and conserves its orthogonality, orientation, and direction. The project obeys the principles of hierarchy of spaces, notions of enclosure, and geometric schemes ruled by a system of proportions (figures 11.9–11.12). Only traditional materials and techniques would be used: earth in the form of *gyang* (rammed-earth) or adobe for certain walls and parapets; stone slabs for the supporting walls, wall bases, and existing walls; river pebbles for the mani walls. Earthen roofs and floors would be supported by a traditional system of beams and columns, following a modular frame defined by the cella's dimensions (see figure 11.7).

If the hermitage came back to life, it would participate in the renewal of the religious and cultural tradition of Lo. Jigme S.P. Bista, son of the Lo Gyalpo, confided that, if Samdrupling were rebuilt, it would be the first modern meditation centre in Lo. The essence of the project thus lies in the will to give the Lopas a possibility to perpetuate a tradition, to create a space propitious to ancient practices and beliefs, while adapting them to the demands of the 21st century.

In this context of constant evolution, new changes related to the development of Lo might well disrupt the balance. The construction of the new road linking Lo Möntang to Jomsom, as well as tourism development since the opening of the region in 1992, are crucial issues in the restoration project of Samdrupling hermitage (figure 11.13). Indeed, the road linking India to Tibet, to Mount Kailash and to Lhasa, will pass about

11.12 Project: Y-Y' section through the cella entrance, courtyards, lamas' room, kitchen, meditation room, and meditation cells.

11.13 East entrance to the Samdrupling enclosure.

3 kilometres east of Samdrupling, and will place Lo at the heart of the geopolitics and economics of the region, after two centuries of relative isolation. In addition, the Lopas contemplate building a "New Lo Möntang" along this road.[8] The development of this new city could have serious consequences for Samdrupling, transforming it from an isolated site to a satellite of the New Lo Möntang, probably attracting tourists in great numbers.

The religious community of the Chödé have understood that tourism is the key to development in Lo, as have a number of other Lopas. The interest of foreign visitors to Lo has resulted in the investment of significant sums of money in the region, in the form of ad hoc aid for various development or conservation projects. This phenomenon has contributed to the revival of the monastic tradition in Lo, but it also raises the issue of its future, and how it may continue to exist. One may wonder if the quiet isolation characterizing meditation places will be compromised by the modern world. The confrontation between tradition and development would place the hermitage project at the heart of a debate: to what extent can meditation, far from bustle and mundane activities, be compatible with the coming of new activities and consequent disturbances?

FIGURE ACKNOWLEDGEMENTS
Unless otherwise credited, illustrations courtesy Maie Kitamura.

NOTES
1   D.P. Jackson, *The Mollas of Mustang: Historical, Religious and Oratorical Traditions of the Nepalese-Tibetan Borderland*, Dharamsala, 1984, p. 136.
2   Ibid., p. 126.
3   R.K. Dhungel, *The Kingdom of Lo (Mustang): A Historical Study*, Kathmandu, 2002, p. 130.
4   H.E. Gyalchung Jigme S.P. Bista, junior raja of Lo, interview of June 28, 2005, Kathmandu.
5   Information from M. Colchen, geologist, CNRS Research Director (Hon.), Professor, Faculty of Sciences, Poitiers University, 2006.
6   A. Chayet, *Art et archéologie du Tibet*, Paris, 1994.
7   Lama Pasang, head monk of Chödé, interview of March 2007.
8   M. Kitamura, *Réanimer un lieu sacré : l'ermitage de Samdrupling, Mustang, nord du Népal; Réhabilitation d'un temple et création d'un centre de méditation,* Travail Personnel de Fin d'Etudes, Ecole Nationale Supérieure d'Architecture de Paris-Belleville, 2006.

List of Phonetic Transcriptions and Equivalent Transliterations of Tibetan Words

Agön Samdrup Rapten (*A mgon bSam grub rab brtan*)

Agön Zangpo (*A mgon bzang po*)

Aku Gochen (*A khu mgo chen*)

Alchi (*A lci*)

Amapel (*A ma dpal, A me dpal*)

amchi (*am chi*, "physician")

Apsé Dungmar (*A bse mdung dmar*)

arga (*ar ka, ar ga*)

Asenggé, Aseng, Ayi Senggé (*A seng ge, A seng, A yi Seng ge*)

Bön (*Bon*)

Chödé (*Chos sde*, "Dharma Centre")

Chödzong (*Chos rdzong*, "Dharma Castle")

chögyel (*chos rgyal*, "righteous king": dharmarāja)

Chögyel Püntsok (*Chos rgyal phun tshogs*)

Chögyel Tendzin (*Chos rgyal bstan 'dzin*)

Chökyi Nyima (*Chos kyi nyi ma*)

Chökyongbum (*Chos skyong 'bum*)

Chönyi Senggé (*Chos nyid seng ge*: Dharmasimha)

Chönyi Zangpo (*Chos nyid bzang po*: Dharmabhadra)

Dampa Bumjé Ö (*Dam pa 'bum rje 'od*)

Dölpo (*Dol po*)

Döndrup Dorjé (*Don grub rdo rje*)

Drakar, Drakar Tekchenling (*Brag dkar Theg chen gling*, "Mahāyāna Island of the White Rock")

Drenpa Namkha (*Dren pa nam mkha'*)

Drigung (*'Bri gung*)

Drongpa (*'Brong pa*)

Drukpa Kagyü (*'Brug pa bKa' brgyud*)

Drukpa Kunle (*'Brug pa Kun legs*)

Dukhang (*'du khang*, assembly hall)

Dzar (*'Dzar*)

Dzokchen (*rDzogs chen*, "Great Perfection")

Dzong (*rDzong*)

Dzongkha (*rDzong kha*)

Garap Dzong (*dGa' rab rdzong*)

Geling (*dGe gling*, "Island of Virtue")

Geluk (*dGe lugs*, "Virtuous School")

Gemi (*Gad smad*)

Gendün Chömpel (*dGe 'dun chos 'phel*)

Gönpa Khang (*dGon pa khang*, "Monastic House")

Gönpo (*mGon po*: Mahākāla)

Gönpuk (*dGon phug*, "Meditation Cave")

Gugé (*Gu ge*)

Gungtang (*Gung thang*)

Gurgön (*mGur mgon*: Pañjara Mahākāla)

Guru Rinpoché (*Guru Rin po che*, "Precious Guru": Padmasambhava)

Gyagar ke du (*rGya gar skad du*, "in Sanskrit")

gyang (*gyang*, wall, clay stamped into moulds)

Gyantsé (*rGyal rtse*, Gyantse)

Gyantsé Penkhor Chödé (*rGyal rtse dPal 'khor chos sde*)

Gyeltsen (*rGyal mtshan*: Dhvaja)

Jamma (*Byams ma*)

Jampa (*Byams pa*: Maitreya)

Jampa Lhakhang (*Byams pa lha khang*, "Temple of Maitreya")

Jampa Tsuklakhang (*Byams pa gtsug lag khang*, "Main Temple of Maitreya": Maitreya Vihāra)

Jampel Dradül (*'Jam dpal dgra 'dul*)

Jampel Senggé (*'Jam dpal seng ge*)

Jikmé Dorjé Dradül (*'Jigs med rdo rje dgra 'dul*)

Jokhang (*Jo khang*, "Temple of the Lord", with reference to an image of Śākyamuni)

Jomsom, Jomosom (*rDzong gsar ma*)

Jonang Künga Drölchok (*Jo nang Kun dga' grol mchog*)

Jowo (*Jo bo*, "Lord": epithet applied to important historical figures and images)

kabum (*bKa' 'bum*, a kind of cave temple stupa)

Kagyü (*bKa' brgyud*, "Transmission of the Word")

Kagyüpa (*bKa' brgyud pa*, "belonging to the Transmission of the Word")

Kak, Kagbeni (*sKag* or *bKag*, "Obstacle")

Kangyur (*bKa' 'gyur*, "Translation of the Word")

Kanying (*bKa' rnying*: Kagyü and Nyingma)

Karu Drupwang Tendzin Rinchen (*Ka ru sGrub dbang bsTan 'dzin rin chen*)

Khachö (*mKha' spyod*, "Celestial Realm")

Kham (*Khams*)

Khyungpo (*Khyung po*)

Könchokling (*dKon mchog gling*, "Jewel Island": Ratnadvīpa)

Künga Nyingpo (*Kun dga' snying po*)

Künga Wangchuk (*Kun dga' dbang phyug*)

Künga Zangpo (*Kun dga' bzang po*: Ānandabhadra)

Künzang Gyelwa Düpa (*Kun bzang rgyal ba 'dus pa*)

Künzang Logyel (*Kun bzang blo rgyal*)

Kutsap Ternga (*sKu tshab gter lnga*)

Kyerang Drakmé (*sKye rang sgrag med*)

Kyirong (*sKyid grong*)

lhakhang (*lha khang*, "temple")

lhatho (*lha tho*, mountain votive cairn)

Lo (*Glo, Blo*)

Lo Gekar (*Glo dGe dkar*, "Pure Virtue of Lo"; also *Glo bo Ges dkar*)

Lopa (*Glo pa, Blo pa*, the people of Lo)

Lowo Khenchen Sönam Lhündrup (*Blo bo mkhan chen bSod nams lhun grub*, "Great Abbot from Lo, Sönam Lhündrup")

Lubrak, Lubra (*Klu brag*, "Nāga [Snake] Crag")

Lubrak Sungma Sinpo Kyerang (*Klu brag srung ma srin po skye rang*)

Lubrakpa (*Klu brag pa*)

Luri (*Klu ri*, "Nāga Hill")

Marpa (*dMar phag*)

Memé (*mes mes*, "Grandfather")

Menri (*sMan ri*)

Mentsi (*sMan rtsi*)

Milarepa (*Mid la ras pa, Mi la ras pa*)

Mipam Püntsok Sherap (*Mi pham phun tshogs shes rab*)

Möntang (*sMon thang*, "Plain of Aspiration")

Namgyel (*rNam rgyal*)

Namkhadrak (*Nam mkha' grags*)

Nampar Gyelwa (*rNam par rgyal ba*, "All-Victorious": Vijaya)

Ngakpa (*sNgags pa*)

Ngari Panchen (*mNga' ris Paṇ chen*,

"Māhapāṇḍita [Great Scholar] of Western Tibet")

Ngor Evam Chönden (*Ngor E vam Chos ldan*)

Ngorchen (*Ngor chen*, title of Künga Zangpo)

Nupchokling (*Nub phyogs gling*, "Western Side Island", or perhaps *Nub tshogs gling*, "Western Settlement Island")

Nyammé Sherap Gyeltsen (*mNyam med Shes rab rgyal mtshan*)

Nyeshang (*sNye shang*)

Nyida Gyelmo (*Nyi zla rgyal mo*, "Queen Nyida")

Nyida Wangmo (*Nyi zla dbang mo*, "Lady Nyida")

Nyingma (*rNying ma*, "Ancient Tradition")

Nyingmapa (*rNying ma pa*, "belonging to the Ancient Tradition")

Öden Barma (*'Od ldan bar ma*)

Pakpa (*'Phags pa*: "Órya")

Pema Karpo (*Padma dkar po*)

Pema tang-yik (*Padma thang yig*)

Pema Wangyel Dorjé (*Padma dBang rgyal rdo rje*)

Penden Lhamo (*dPal ldan Lha mo*: Śrī Devī, namely Rematī)

Penkhor Chödé (*dPal 'khor chos sde*, "Dharma Centre of the Glorious Enclave")

Piyang (*Phyi dbang*)

Püntsok Sherap (see Mipam Püntsok Sherap)

Püntsokling Lhakang (*Phun tshogs gling lha khang*, "Temple of the Island of Prosperity")

Purang (*Pu hrang*)

rikpa (*rig pa*: jñana, knowledge)

Rinchen Zangpo (*Rin chen bzang po*)

Rindzinling (*Rig 'dzin gling*, "Vidyādhara Island": Vidyādharadvīpa)

Ronggom Tokmé Zhikpo (*Rong sgom rTog med zhig po*)

Saga (*Sa dga'*)

Sakya (*Sa skya*)

Sakyapa (*Sa skya pa*, "belonging to Sakya")

Sakyong Ayi Senggé (*Sa skyong A yi Seng ge*)

Samdrup Dorjé (*bSam grub rdo rje*)

Samdrup Pembar (*bSam grub dpal 'bar*)

Samdrup Rapten (*bSam grub rab brtan*)

Samdrupling (*bSam grub gling*, "Island of the Fulfilment of Aspirations")

Samyè (*bSam yas*, "Inconceivable")

Sanggyè Zangpo (*Sangs rgyas bzang po*)

Sanggyèpel (*Sangs rgyas dpal*)

Shakya Chokden (*Shakya mChog ldan*)

Shé (*Shel*)

Shekar (*Shel dkar*)

Shentön Yeshé Lotrö (*gShen ston Ye shes blo gros*)

Sherap Gyeltsen (*Shes rab rgyal mtshan*)

Sherap Lama (*Shes rab Bla ma*)

Sherap Miwo (see Tönpa Sherap Miwo)

Sherap Rinchen (*Shes rab rin chen*)

Shöyül (*Shod yul*)

Sipè Gyelmo (*Srid pa'i rgyal mo*)

Sönam Gyeltsen (*bSod nams rgyal mtshan*)

Sönam Lhündrup (*bSod nams lhun grub*)

Songtsen Gampo (*Srong brtsan sgam po*)

tangka (*thang ka*, generally referring to a painted scroll)

Tapiritsa (*Ta pi hri tsa*)

Tazik (*rTags gzigs*)

Te (*gTer/lTe*)

Tengyur (*bsTan 'gyur*)

Tenpè Gyeltsen (*bsTan pa'i rgyal mtshan*)

tiklé (*thig le*: bindu, "drop")

Tingkhyu (*Ting khyu*)

Tokmé Zhikpo (*rTog med zhig po*)

Tönpa Sherap Miwo (*sTon pa gShen rab Mi bo*)

Tönpa Yang-rap (*sTon pa Yang rab*)

Trakpuk (*brag phug*, rock cave)

Trashi Geling (*bKra shis dge gling*, "Island of Auspicious Happiness and Virtue")

Trashi Gyeltsen (*bKra shis rgyal mtshan*)

Trashigön (*bKra shis mgon*)

Trashilhünpo (*bKra shis lhum po*)

Tropuk (*Khro phug*)

Trülnang (*'Phrul snang*)

Tsang Nyön Heruka (*gTsang smyon He ru ka*, "Heruka Madman from Tsang")

Tsangchen Trashigön (*Tshangs chen bkra shis mgon*: Mahā-Brahmā Maṅgala-Mahākāla)

Tsaparang (*rTsa brang*)

Tsarang (*gTsang rang*)

Tsechen Shedrupling (*brTse chen shes grub gling*, "Island of the Accomplishment of Kindness")

Tsongkhapa (*Tsong kha pa*)

Tsoshar, Tsokshar, Choshar (*mTsho shar* or *Tshogs shar*)

Tsuk, Chusang (*Tshug*)

Tsuktorlak (*gTsug gtor lags*)

Tukché, Trutsé (*Gru rtse*)

tülku (*sprul sku*: nirmāṇakāya)

Tupchen (*Thub chen*: Mahāmuni)

Tupten Dargyeling (*Thub bstan dar rgyas gling*, "Island of the Spreading and Flourishing of Mahāmuni's Teachings")

Tupten Sampel Ling (*Thub bstan bsam 'phel gling*, "Wish-Fulfilling Island of Mahāmuni's Teachings")

uchen (*dbu can*, "headed", referring to block letters)

Wangyel Dorjé (see Pema Wangyel Dorjé)

Yantön Sherap Gyeltsen (*Yang ston Shes rab rgyal mtshan*)

Yarlung (*Yar klungs*)

Yatsé (*Ya tshe*)

Zangpo Lhajin (*bZang po lha sbyin*)

Zhalu (*Zhwa lu*)

Zhangzhung (*Zhang zhung*)

Zhangzhung Meri (*Zhang zhung me ri*)

Zhönnupel (*gZhon nu dpal*)

Index

Contributors

Erberto Lo Bue, the editor of this volume, is Associate Professor at the University of Bologna, where he teaches history of Indian and Central Asian art as well as classical Tibetan at the Department of Linguistic and Oriental Studies. He has carried out fieldwork in Nepal since 1972 and Tibet since 1987. Most of his publications are related to Tibetan and Himalayan art.

John Harrison is a historic-buildings architect, and an associate of the Oriental Institute, University of Oxford. As a student of Tibetan architecture he has spent a long time in the Himalaya (including Mustang), documenting and repairing traditional buildings in Ladakh, Nepal, and Tibet.

Luigi Fieni is scientific consultant for conservation and restoration at John Sanday Associates, Kathmandu. Of the American Himalayan Foundation's restoration projects in which he has been involved, the most relevant is the one carried out in Mustang at the temples of Tupchen and Jampa, and monasteries of Tupten Dargyeling and Ghar from 1999, and directed by him since 2004.

Helmut F. Neumann is a scientist with a simultaneous lifelong interest in art history. He has carried out studies of Asian art history at Harvard University together with his wife **Heidi A. Neumann**. From 1972 they made yearly visits to Himalayan countries, concentrating on art-historically relevant sites. Their first publication on the Luri Stupa and its wall paintings appeared in 1994. Since 1990, they have regularly made research trips to Tibet, and contributions at academic conferences, with over 20 publications on early wall paintings in the temples and caves of Western and Central Tibet.

Amy Heller is an art historian and Tibetologist, affiliated with the Tibetan studies team UMR 8155 of the National Scientific Research Centre in Paris since 1986. She is the author of more than 60 articles and five books, most recently, *Hidden Treasures of the Himalayas: Tibetan Manuscripts, Paintings and Sculptures of Dolpo* (Chicago, 2009). Visiting Professor at the Centre for Tibetan Studies, Sichuan University 2007–10, she has travelled extensively throughout Tibet and the Himalaya, as well as along the Silk Road, to study Tibetan art and archaeology in situ.

Chiara Bellini has studied the history of Indian and Tibetan art at the University of Bologna since 1999, focusing on the history of wall painting, and carrying out fieldwork in Ladakh and Nepal, including Lo (Mustang). She obtained her PhD in Indology and Tibetology with a thesis on 14th–16th-century Ladakhi murals. She is currently preparing a monograph on the history of Buddhist art in Ladakh in collaboration with Erberto Lo Bue.

Maie Kitamura has worked in the field of architectural conservation for the Kathmandu Valley Preservation Trust and carried out fieldwork in Mustang. She graduated from the School of Paris-Belleville with a thesis on the structure and symbolism of the urban architecture of Möntang, the capital of Mustang.